FOR MALCOLM

MALCOLM X, FEBRUARY, 1965.

(Photo: Courtesy of James D. Wilson, Custom
Photography, Detroit.)

TO MRS. BETTY SHABAZZ

BOOKS BY DUDLEY RANDALL

Poem Counterpoem (with Margaret Danner)

For Malcolm: Poems on the Life and the Death of Malcolm X
(edited with Margaret G. Burroughs)

BOOKS BY MARGARET BURROUGHS

Jasper the Drummin' Boy (Children's)

Did You Feed My Cow? (Children's)

Whip Me Whop Me Pudding (Children's)

For Malcolm: Poems on the Life and the Death of Malcolm X
(edited with Dudley Randall)

FOR MALCOLM

POEMS ON THE LIFE
AND THE DEATH
OF MALCOLM X

Edited by
DUDLEY RANDALL
and
MARGARET G. BURROUGHS

Preface and Eulogy by
OSSIE DAVIS

With Biography; Bibliography; and Photographs
and Biographical Notes of Authors

BROADSIDE PRESS
12651 Old Mill Place
Detroit, Michigan 48238

Library of Congress Card Number 74-78642
Manufactured in the United States of America

CONTENTS

Acknowledgements

The editors thank all the poets included in this book for their contributions. We are grateful to George Breitman for items from his bibliography on Malcolm X, and to Larry Neal, Hoyt W. Fuller, and all others who contributed items.

We thank Mrs. Azarea Wright for valuable assistance in preparing the manuscript for the printer.

We give special thanks to the following persons whose donations helped to pay for the printing of this book: Mrs. Grace Lee Boggs, Sylvester Britton, Joe C. Brown, Mrs. Thelma Muhammad, Wilberforce Jones, W. C. Anas Luqman, Robert Randall, Mildred Stennis, and Dr. Robert Perkins.

We are grateful to the following writers and publications for permission to reprint these works:

Ossie Davis. "Why I Eulogized Malcolm X," and "Eulogy of Malcolm X." From *The Autobiography of Malcolm X*. With Alex Haley, New York, Grove Press, Copyright (C) 1965 by Alex Haley and Betty Shabazz; (C) 1965 by Roger Price.

Le Graham. "The Black Shining Prince." From *The Black Narrator*, by Le Graham. Distributed by Vaughn's Bookstore, 12123 Dexter Avenue, Detroit. Copyright (C) Le Graham 1966.

LeRoi Jones. "A Poem for Black Hearts." From *Negro Digest,* September 1965. Copyright (C) 1965 by LeRoi Jones. Reprinted by permission of the Sterling Lord Agency.

K. William Kgositsile. "Brother Malcolm's Echo." From *Poems Now,* edited by Hettie Jones, New York, Kulchur Press, (C) Copyright 1966.

David Llorens. "One Year Ago." From *Negro Digest,* February 1966. (C) Copyright 1966, by the Johnson Publishing Company, Inc.

Patricia. "Two for Malcolm." From *Freedomways,* Spring 1966. Copyright 1966, by Freedomways Associates, Inc.

John Sinclair. "The Destruction of America." From *This Is Our Music,* by John Sinclair. Detroit, Artists' Workshop Press. Copyright (C) by John Sinclair 1965.

THE LIFE OF MALCOLM X

Malcolm X was born May 19, 1925 in Omaha, Nebraska. His father, the Reverend Earl Little, was a Baptist minister and an organizer for Marcus Garvey's Universal Negro Improvement Association. His mother, Louise Little, was born in Grenada, British West Indies. Her father, whom she had never seen, was white.

Malcolm was his father's seventh child. His father had three children by a previous marriage, Ella, Earl, and Mary. His oldest full brother was Wilfred. Then Hilda and Philbert were born. After Malcolm's birth, his family moved to Milwaukee, where Reginald was born. After a short stay there, the family moved to Lansing, Michigan.

His father continued organizing for the U.N.I.A., and was threatened by the Black Legionnaires, a Ku Klux Klan type organization. Shortly after Yvonne, his youngest sister, was born in 1929 his house was set on fire by two white men who were shot at by his father. The firemen and policemen came and stood by and watched his house burn to the ground. Afterward, the police used to come and search the house for the pistol with which his father had defended it.

The family moved to a house on the outskirts of East Lansing, home of Michigan State University. They were harassed so much that they had to move out of town, into the country. His father built the four-room house himself. Malcolm attended the Pleasant Grove school outside the city. Meanwhile, two more brothers, Wesley and Robert, were born.

In 1931 his father was killed. His skull was crushed. His body was found on the street car tracks almost cut in two. Malcolm believed that he had been attacked by whites and then laid on the tracks for a street car to run over. One of the two insurance companies refused to pay his mother, and this disturbed her and helped to lead to her mental breakdown. She developed the habit of talking to herself.

Wilfred quit school and took a job. His mother worked, but when the people learned she was a Negro, they would fire her. Malcolm and Philbert shot rabbits, trapped muskrats, and killed frogs to help out.

The State Welfare people came to the home looking and asking questions as if the family were not people. Once they called his mother "crazy" for refusing a gift of pork. Finally in 1937 they took her to the State Mental Hospital in Kalamazoo where she stayed until she left the hospital to live with Philbert in 1963. Malcolm and his brothers and sisters were placed under the custody of Judge McClellan in Lansing. Malcolm stayed with some neighbors, the Gohannas, and went to Lansing West Junior High School.

Expelled from school for putting a tack on his teacher's seat, he was to be sent to the reform school, but instead he was kept in the detention home run in Mason by Mr. and Mrs. Swerlin. They were a kindly couple and liked Malcolm, but they treated him like a mascot and not a person, talking about him and about "niggers" in his presence. He entered the seventh grade in Mason Junior High School, where he played on the basketball team and was elected class president. He was one of the three brightest students in the school, but when he told Mr. Ostrowski, his English teacher, that he wanted to be a lawyer, Mr. Ostrowski said, "That's no realistic goal for a nigger. Why don't you plan on carpentry?"

In his history book there was only one paragraph about the Negro. His history teacher skipped over that by cracking the joke that all Negroes had feet so big they left a hole in the ground when they walked. When he finished the eighth grade, Malcolm went to live with his sister Ella in Roxbury, a suburb of Boston.

There, he got a job as shoeshine boy in the Roseland State Ballroom, through Shorty, a home boy from Lansing, whom he met in a poolroom. He learned the 'hustles' of selling liquor, reefers, and slipping addresses and tele-

phone numbers of black prostitutes to the white men.
He learned to drink, gamble, and smoke reefers, and
began playing the numbers for a dollar a day. He learned to Lindy-hop, and quit his job so that he could dance
at the Roseland. At a Roseland dance he met the blonde
Sophia who became his girl and gave him money and
status in black Roxbury. At sixteen he got a job selling
sandwiches on the railroad between Boston and New
York and became acquainted with Harlem. Fired
from the railroad, he got a job as a waiter at Small's
Paradise in New York. The cooks, bartenders, and cus-
tomers schooled him in the history of Harlem and in
the various hustles. He listened to the yarns of hustlers
like Sammy the Pimp, Dollarbill, Fewclothes, Jump-
steady, and Cadillac Drake. He lost his job at Small's
when he gave a lonely-looking soldier, who was a
Federal agent, the address of a prostitute. He then
took up the racket of selling reefers. When it became
too hot for him in New York, he caught the train and
sold reefers to traveling musicians. When he returned
to New York, he resorted to stickups and burglaries.
His next job was as a messenger for a numbers man.
Then he became a steerer for wealthy whites with un-
usual sexual appetites. Then he worked for Hymie, a
real estate and business speculator. When he got into
trouble with Italian gangsters, two other hustlers, and
the police all at the same time, he left New York and
went back to Boston with Shorty. There he began a
series of burglaries with Shorty, Sophia and her younger
sister, and a mulatto named Rudy. He was caught when
he had a stolen watch repaired, and sentenced to ten
years. He was not yet twenty-one.

He stayed first at Charlestown State Prison, where
his behavior earned him many stays in solitary and the
name of Satan. He took correspondence courses in
English and Latin and tried to read library books. He
was transferred to Concord Prison and in 1948 to Nor-
folk Prison Colony which had a good library. In his

hustler's life he had hardly been able to read and write.
Now he began copying the whole dictionary to learn to
write and to understand the meaning of words. He read
in every spare moment, sometimes as much as fifteen
hours a day. After lights were out, he read by the glow
of a corridor light until three or four in the morning.
This so hurt his eyes that he had to wear glasses. He
practiced debating and found it exciting. In his reading
he concentrated on the history of the Negro and learned
how the white man had exploited and brainwashed him.

His brother Reginald introduced him to the religion
of Islam. Its condemnation of the white man gave Malcolm an explanation of the hardships of the Negro race.
He became a convert, and wrote to Elijah Muhammad
every day. His last year of prison was spent in Charlestown Prison. In August 1952 he was released on parole
in custody of his brother Wilfred in Detroit who man-
aged a furniture store. Malcolm worked as a salesman.
Later he worked at Gar Wood and at the Lincoln-Mer-
cury Division of the Ford Motor Company. On Labor
Day he visited Chicago with a caravan from Detroit
and met Elijah. Elijah later appointed him assistant
minister of Detroit, and establisher of temples. He
established new temples in Boston, Philadelphia, New
York, Springfield, Massachussets, Hartford, Atlanta, and
other cities. Because of Elijah's affliction with asthma,
he gave Malcolm more and more responsibilities. Malcolm became known as the Nation of Islam's number
two man, and spoke often on radio, television, and at
colleges. He began to sense jealousy among some of
the other leaders, and noticed that a news blackout
was being imposed on him.

In the meantime, Malcolm had met a young nursing
student, Betty X, who taught the women of Islam. Oc-
casionally he would speak to her or ask her questions
about her work. Once when he was in Detroit, he called
her long distance in New York and asked her to marry

him. She answered yes, and they were married January 14, 1958 in Lansing.

About the time of his news blackout he learned that some of the secretaries of Elijah had become pregnant. He spoke to Elijah about it, and Elijah told him that prophecy was being fulfilled. When President Kennedy was assassinated, Malcolm said, "the chickens have come home to roost." Elijah told him not to make any public statements for six months. Malcolm kept silence, but felt that his position was becoming increasingly worse. Finally he decided to visit Mecca.

He made two trips to Africa, and each time was treated with courtesy, respect and brotherhood by the Africans, many of whom would be regarded in America as white men. This caused him to revise his belief that all white men were evil.

In March 1964 he announced to the press that he would form his own organization, the Organization of Afro-American Unity. He established a mosque for the Islam religion called the Muslim Mosque, Inc., but the OAAU would concentrate on political and civil rights activities, and would be open to Negroes of all faiths. He held meetings in the Audubon Ballroom in Harlem.

In the meantime the Nation of Islam was suing to dispossess him of his house in Long Island. During his affiliation with them he had not tried to save or accumulate any money, and had no insurance. On Sunday, February 14th, his home was bombed, but no one was injured. He complained to his associates that the police did not pay any attention to his requests for protection. On the other hand, Deputy Police Commissioner Walter said he refused police protection. After the bombing Malcolm said that the acts against him were greater than could be done by the Nation of Islam.

On Sunday the 21st of February, 1965, there was an OAAU meeting scheduled in the Audubon Ballroom. Malcolm had given up Elijah's practice of having everyone searched before admission. There was an alterca-

tion near the front, which attracted everyone's attention. Malcolm said, "Hold it! Hold it! Don't get excited.
Let's cool it, brothers." Some men in the front row
stood up and fired at him. He fell over backward. People ran out, or tried to catch the assassins. Betty Shabazz
ran to the stage and kneeled over Malcolm. She said,
"They killed him!" Someone tried to apply mouth-to-
mouth respiration. Two policemen driving by appre-
hended a man being beaten by the crowd. The man was
Talmadge Hayer. (Later Norman 3X Butler and Thomas
15X Johnson were arrested and indicted for the murder
of Malcolm X along with Hayer. They were given life
sentences for first degree murder.)

Someone got a stretcher from the Columbia-Pres-
byterian Hospital and Malcolm was placed in it and carried to the hospital. Surgeons cut into his chest to mas-
sage his heart. At 3:30 p.m. they gave up. His body
was taken to the New York City Medical Examiner's
office for autopsy, where it was announced that his
death was caused by shotgun wounds in his heart. There
were thirteen wounds in his chest from shotgun pellets,
and .38 and .45 caliber bullet wounds in his thighs and
legs. His body was taken to the Unity Funeral Home,
and lay in state from Tuesday, February 23 through
Friday, February 26. About 22,000 people filed by to
see his body.

Several churches, including the Abyssinian Baptist
Church, the Williams C.M.E. Church, and the Refuge
Temple of the Church of Our Lord Jesus Christ refused
to take the funeral. At last Bishop Alvin A. Childs of
the Faith Temple, Church of God in Christ accepted the
funeral. About six hundred and fifty people attended
the funeral, where actor Ossie Davis read the eulogy.
A funeral procession of about ninety cars followed the
body to Ferncliff Cemetery in Ardsley, New York, where
Malcolm X was buried February 27, 1965.

INTRODUCTION

Hearing Margaret Walker read her poem on Malcolm X at the Fisk University Writers' Conference in April 1966, we were reminded of the great number of poems that had been written in his memory, and we decided to make a selection from them and to publish it.

At the last session of the Conference, we announced plans for the anthology. David Llorens, then assistant editor of **Negro Digest,** promised to announce the book in the magazine. A few days after the Conference, the first poem arrived, sent by Edward Richer from Florida, who wrote that he had been in the audience that night.

Poems and words of encouragement began to come in. "Your highly laudable project." "The book's a fine idea." "I wish you the best of luck with the collection and compliment you for putting it together." "I wish you good luck in your worthwhile attempt to publish thoughts on our tragic loss of Malcolm X." "I have often wondered if there was anyone bold enough to compile such an anthology." "Your letter regarding the anthology in memory to Brother Malcolm X was received with great admiration and gratitude."

There was praise for Malcolm. "I shall look forward to reading the volume since I greatly admired Malcolm X." "I hope (my poem) is worthy of both the memory of Malcolm and the anthology. This is one of the rare times I feel moved to be modest about my work." "It goes without saying that Brother Malcolm will always stand high in my world of truly great men."

As the poems came in we noticed that they grouped themselves by certain themes. We have arranged them in the same pattern in the book. The poems are divided into four sections: The Life, The Death, The Rage, and The Aftermath.

The list of poets is an honor roll of younger poets. Well-known and prize-winning poets like Gwendolyn Brooks, LeRoi Jones, Robert Hayden, Margaret Walker, Margaret Danner contributed. Prolific and much-published poets like Clarence Major, John Sinclair, James Worley, and Ted Joans sent in poems. Talented young poets like Mari Evans, Julia Fields, Sonia Sanchez, David Henderson, Raymond Patterson, Helen Quigless, Bobb Hamilton, and Larry Neal contributed. There were also poems by unknown and unpublished poets. "One Year Ago," by David Llorens, which heads the second section, was his first published poem. James Lucas's ballad-like "Caution" is his first poem to be published. Christine Johnson, Reginald Wilson, Margaret Burroughs, and others who had seldom published poems contributed.

The distribution is from Ted Joans in Holland and clusters of big-city poets (to name only a few) like New York poets Patricia McIlnay, Jay Wright, Carmin Auld Goulbourne, Theodore Horne, and Willie Kgositsile, exiled from South Africa; Detroit poets Oliver LaGrone, Joyce Whitsitt, Le Graham, and George Norman; Chicago poets Kent Foreman, Conrad Kent Rivers, Zack Gilbert, to isolated poets like Margaret Walker in Mississippi, Nanina Alba in Alabama, Etheridge Knight who writes from Indiana State Prison, and Marcella Caine in Portland, Oregon. A large city like Philadelphia is represented only by the songwriter, Bill Frederick. Two California magazines, **Black Dialogue** and **Soulbook,** are represented, but by their New York editors Edward Spriggs and Bobb Hamilton. **Freedomways, Negro Digest,** and the books **This Is Our Music, Poems Now,** and **The Black Narrator** also supply poems.

James Patterson, an Afro-Russian poet whose great grandfather was an American slave, sent a Russian and an English version of a poem from Moscow.

The styles vary from the clipped syllables of Gwendolyn Brooks and the glittering phrases of Robert Hayden, from the dense-packed images of Carmin Auld Goulbourne and Oliver LaGrone, to the experimental punctuation and phrasing of LeRoi Jones, John Sinclair, and Le Graham, and the hip dialect of Ted Joans and Etheridge Knight. There are many Semitic words, because of Malcolm's Semitic religion. The figures apostrophized by the poets are not the slave-holding Washington or Jefferson, but freedom fighters Toussaint L'Ouverture, Gabriel Prosser, Denmark Vesey, Nat Turner, and leaders in our own time Marcus Garvey, W.E.B. Du Bois, Robert Williams, Patrice Lumumba, and LeRoi Jones.

The theme which recurs in many of the poems, and which recalls the theme of Ossie Davis's preface, is that Malcolm was a man, in spite of white America's effort to emasculate the Blackman. Gwendolyn Brooks says, "He had the hawkman's eyes./ We gasped. We saw the maleness." Joyce Whitsitt says, "You were the brilliant embodiment/ Of elusive manhood." George Norman says, "You were our symbol — of black manhood."

John Oliver Killens says in **Black Man's Burden** that if a black man walked with his wife in a southern country fair, and some drunken white slapped his wife on the buttocks, he had three choices. He could pretend he didn't see it, he could grin, or he could die. In such situations some black men have chosen to die, but many more have lived, but not without a diminution of spirit, of soul, of self-respect. What they admire in Malcolm is that he didn't bite his tongue, but spelled out the evil done by the white man and told him to go to hell. There is no black man, regardless of his agreement or disagreement with Malcolm's politics, goals, or racial theories, whether he's a serf in Mississippi, a cat on the corner in Chicago, or a black bourgeois in Westchester, who didn't feel a stiffening of his spine and pride in his blackness when he saw or heard Malcolm take on all comers, and rout them. There are some who feel threatened by the taking of full manhood rights by the Blackman. Malcolm was a man, and for being a man he was murdered.

Detroit   Dudley Randall

Chicago   Margaret Burroughs

November 1966

PREFACE

WHY I EULOGIZED MALCOLM X

(The text of the Eulogy is in the Appendix)

BY OSSIE DAVIS

*One of the first persons to express shock, horror,
and sorrow over the fatal shooting of Malcolm X,
February, 1965, was actor-playwright Ossie Davis.
At Malcolm's funeral, Mr. Davis read the eulogy in
which he called the slain black nationalist leader—
"Our Black Shining Prince." Mr. Davis wrote the
following in response to a magazine editor's question:
Why did you eulogize Malcolm X?*

You are not the only person curious to know why
I would eulogize a man like Malcolm X. Many who know
and respect me have written letters. Of these letters I
am proudest of those from a sixth-grade class of young
white boys and girls who asked me to explain. I ap-
preciate your giving me this chance to do so.

You may anticipate my defense somewhat by con-
sidering the following fact: no Negro has yet asked me
that question. (My pastor in Grace Baptist Church where
I teach Sunday school preached a sermon about Malcolm in which he called him a "giant in a sick world.")
Every one of the many letters I got from my own people
lauded Malcolm as a man, and commended me for having spoken at his funeral.

At the same time — and this is important — most
all of them took special pains to disagree with much
or all of what Malcolm said and what he stood for. That
is, with one singing exception, they all, every last, black,
glory-hugging one of them, knew that Malcolm—whatever else he was or was not—**Malcolm was a man!**

White folks do not need anybody to remind them
that they are men. We do! This was his one incontro-
vertible benefit to his people.

Protocol and common sense require that Negroes
stand back and let the white man speak up for us, defend us, and lead us from behind the scene in our fight.
This is the essence of Negro politics. But Malcolm said
to hell with that! Get up off your knees and fight your
own battles. That's the way to win back your self-
respect. That's the way to make the white man respect
you. And if he won't let you live like a man, he certainly
can't keep you from dying like one!

Malcolm, as you can see, was refreshing excitement;
he scared hell out of the rest of us, bred as we are to
caution, to hypocrisy in the presence of white folks, to
the smile that never fades. Malcolm knew that every
white man in America profits directly or indirectly from
his position vis-á-vis Negroes, profits from racism even
though he does not practice it or believe it.

He also knew that every Negro who did not challenge
on the spot every instance of racism, overt or covert,
committed against him and his people, who chose instead to swallow his spit and go on smiling, was an
Uncle Tom and a traitor, without balls or guts, or any
other commonly accepted aspects of manhood!

Now, we knew all these things as well as Malcolm
did, but we also knew what happened to people who
stick their necks out and say them. And if all the lies
we tell ourselves by way of extenuation were put into
print, it would constitute one of the great chapters in
the history of man's justifiable cowardice in the face
of other men.

But Malcolm kept snatching our lies away. He kept
shouting the painful truth we whites and blacks did
not want to hear from all the housetops. And he
woldn't stop for love nor money.

You can imagine what a howling, shocking nuisance
this man was to both Negroes and whites. Once Malcolm

fastened on you, you could not escape. He was one of the most fascinating and charming men I have ever met, and never hesitated to take his attractiveness and beat you to death with it. Yet his irritation, though painful to us, was most salutary. He would make you angry as hell, but he would also make you proud. It was impossible to remain defensive and apologetic about being a Negro in his presence. He wouldn't let you. And you always left his presence with the sneaky suspicion that maybe, after all, you were a man!

But in explaining Malcolm, let me take care not to explain him away. He had been a criminal, an addict, a pimp, and a prisoner; a racist, and a hater, he had really believed the white man was a devil. But all this had changed. Two days before his death, in commenting to Gordon Parks about his past life he said: "That was a mad scene. The sickness and madness of those days! I'm glad to be free of them."

And Malcolm was free. No one who knew him before and after his trip to Mecca could doubt that he had completely abandoned racism, separatism, and hatred. But he had not abandoned his shock-effect statements, his bristling agitation for immediate freedom in this country not only for blacks, but for everybody.

And most of all, in the area of race relations, he still delighted in twisting the white man's tail, and in making Uncle Toms, compromisers and accommodationists— I deliberately include myself—thoroughly ashamed of the urbane and smiling hypocrisy we practice merely to exist in a world whose values we both envy and despise.

But even had Malcolm not changed, he would still have been a relevant figure on the American scene, standing in relation as he does, to the "responsible" civil rights leaders, just about where John Brown stood in relation to the "responsible" abolitionist in the fight against slavery. Almost all disagreed with Brown's mad and fanatical tactics which led him foolishly to attack a Federal arsenal at Harpers Ferry, to lose two sons there, and later to be hanged for treason.

Yet, today the world, and especially the Negro people, proclaim Brown not a traitor, but a hero and a martyr in a noble cause. So in future, I will not be surprised if men come to see that Malcolm X was, within his own limitations, and in his own inimitable style, also a martyr in that cause.

But there is much controversy still about this most controversial American, and I am content to wait for history to make the final decision.

But in personal judgment, there is no appeal from instinct. I knew the man personally, and however much I disagreed with him, I never doubted that Malcolm X, even when he was wrong, was always that rarest thing in the world among us Negroes: a true man.

And if, to protect my relations with the many good white folks who make it possible for me to earn a fairly good living in the entertainment industry, I was too chicken, too cautious, to admit that fact when he was alive, I thought at least that now, when all the white folks are safe from him at last, I could be honest with myself enough to lift my hat for one final salute to that brave, black, ironic gallantry, which was his style and hallmark, that shocking zing of fire-and-be-damned-to-you, so absolutely absent in every other Negro man I know, which brought him, too soon, to his death.

Reprinted from *The Autobiography of Malcolm X*
Copyright © 1965, Grove Press
by permission of Ossie Davis

FOR MALCOLM:

The Life

MALCOLM X

FOR DUDLEY RANDALL

Original.
Hence ragged-round,
Hence rich-robust.

He had the hawk-man's eyes.
We gasped. We saw the maleness.
The maleness raking out and making guttural the air
And pushing us to walls.

And in a soft and fundamental hour
A sorcery devout and vertical
Beguiled the world.

He opened us —
Who was a key.

Who was a man.

GWENDOLYN BROOKS

MY BROTHER MALCOLM

I see you now
Standing tall,
Erect, fearless,
Speaking with voice so loud
Accusing, condemning
Wrong.
Wrong against the Brother,
Who has suffered
So long, so long,
So long.

I hear you, Malcolm.
You with perfect diction.
Fire in your voice
Fire in your eyes
Saying the things
That the Brother and Sister
Long to hear.

I feel the warmth of your
Handclasp.
The true feeling of friendship
And brotherly love.
I feel the tenderness of your love
And sincerity.
Truly you were my brother,
And brother of all black mankind.
Ah! Brother, why did you have
To die?

                                    CHRISTINE C. JOHNSON

THE INSURGENT

Give me my freedom
lest I die
for pride runs through my veins
not blood
and principles
support me so that
I
with lifted head see
Liberty . . . . not sky!
For I am he who
dares to say
I shall be Free, or dead —
today. . .

                                    MARI EVANS

MY ACE OF SPADES

MALCOLM X SPOKE TO ME and sounded you
Malcolm X said this to me & THEN TOLD you that!
Malcolm X whispered in my ears but SCREAMED
    on you!
Malcolm X praised me & thus condemned you
Malcolm X smiled at me & sneered at you
Malcolm X made me proud & so you got scared
Malcolm X told me to HURRY & you began to worry
Malcolm X sang to me but GROWLED AT YOU!!
Malcolm X words freed me & they frightened you
Malcolm X tol' it lak it DAMN SHO' IS!!
Malcolm X said that everybody will be F R E E ! !
Malcolm X told both of us the T R U T H . . . . . .
                          now didn't he?
                          TED JOANS

THE COST

Soft answers turn away, they say,
Wrath. True perhaps. But at what cost?
How often wrath, thus answered, veers
Smirkingly sure its point is made.
(Wrath smirking battens unassuaged
And preens to fright another day.)
Is a wrath turned smug to be preferred
To one confronted, challenged and—
If unquellable— endured
In the dignity that stanchness gives
To those whose cause will not defer?
(Even wrath that overpowers
Is lessoned and diminished by
A victim that is adamant.)
Soft answers, sponges, take offense
Into every masochistic pore
And spongelike hold it hidden neat
In lieu of the gusts that courage gulps.

(While the tide that lordly forced the pores
Ebbs in contemptuous certainty,
Its flotsam stays to fret each cell
Of the seeming-same soft-answerer.)

JAMES WORLEY

THEY FEARED THAT HE BELIEVED

The press boys tried to erase
what he said. Smear it. Change it.
This meant that he no longer
trusted the lies of the times.
Too strong in his manhood.
This meant that reason was no longer reason.
What he said showed them
he did not see the world through
THEIR eyes. This frightened them:
And his death came.
Was not permitted by magic to take;
he was not here long enough
for the final exams—so
no showdown came: because the cops
and the lie still lived.

CLARENCE MAJOR

MALCOLM X, A LOVER OF THE GRASS ROOTS

Dear Pots,
How much love did you, (who hate the hatred
that he hated back at haters) feel

for the greys who jeered the black kindergarten
front guard (forever scratched, now) as it
trudged the long and hate-lined campus yard
to school?

Did you love your hate filled grey brothers
or did your 'soul' reel for the brave babies
and their scar tissued black mothers?

In these times of change-over into the New Day,
hypocrisy, a multi-colored snake
in a patterned, but briar hedge
is threshing against its shedding.

And Malcolm X, having outgrown the tricks
of this briar trade was so churned
over the stunting of the grass roots of us
that he dared to say, aloud,"I hate,"

thrusting the points his dying proved,
for as a precocious twig, scratching
above the line of the landscaped thorns,
he was snapped off.

I saw him with those he called his own,
His growling laughter
at the sinister absurdity of the thorned plan
rumbled with such force through the window
of a fought-for auditorium
that it drew me from the house next door.

And there chafed a deeply loving Malcolm X
imploring us to stand, not bow, walk, not
hesitate. To try his way out.

And we could all feel and follow the ache
of his wounds as the briars
of our suffering festered in him.

As for hate,
life was already trending him
toward a more livable estate.

So, you, from grey through black,
who lack Malcolm's mettle, consider,
before you miscall this uncompromising kettle.

                                    MARGARET DANNER

JUNGLE FLOWER

Jungle colors,
Fluted and starred,
Blossom at night
Without regard
For the dying blight
Long overgrown
Of rotting log
And crumbling stone.

As a ghetto child
He blossomed and grew
Without regard
For the blight he knew
That hatred is black
And fear is white,
But death flowered redly
One awful night.

MARCELLA CAINE

BROTHER MALCOLM: WASTE LIMIT

He said A REAL REVOLUTION
to change the structure
of the society: money in the bank
and not in the dresser drawer
he meant
        he also meant a lack of killing
of the self
which the peak of white society
imposed on the bottom, the back porch
of the empire

He said A REAL REVOLUTION
for men No longer the white interpreter
of things for the world
of non-whites No longer the garbage cans
by the front door
        No longer the petty arguments
between the victims

But he did not live to see Unity
the pettiness got him with metal.

CLARENCE MAJOR

MALCOLM X—AN AUTOBIOGRAPHY

I am the Seventh Son of the Son
who was also the Seventh.
I have drunk deep of the waters of my ancestors
have traveled the soul's journey towards cosmic
        harmony
the Seventh Son.
Have walked slick avenues
and seen grown men, fall, to die in a blue doom
of death and ancestral agony,
have seen old men glide, shadowless, feet barely
touching the pavements.

I sprung out of the Midwestern plains
the bleak Michigan landscape wearing the slave name—
Malcolm Little.
Saw a brief vision in Lansing, when I was seven, and in
my mother's womb heard the beast cry of death,
a landscape on which white robed figures ride, and my
Garvey father silhouetted against the night-fire, gun
        in hand
form outlined against a panorama of violence.

Out of the midwestern bleakness, I sprang, pushed
        eastward,
past shack on country nigger shack, across the
        wilderness
of North America.
I hustler. I pimp. I unfulfilled black man
bursting with destiny.
New York city Slim called me Big Red,
and there was no escape, close nights of the smell
        of death.
Pimp. Hustler. The day fills these rooms.

I am talking about New York. Harlem.
talking about the neon madness.
talking about ghetto eyes and nights

about death oozing across the room. Small's paradise.
talking about cigarette butts, and rooms smelly
     with white
sex flesh, and dank sheets, and being on the run.
talking about cocaine illusions, about stealing
     and selling.
talking about these New York cops who smell of
     blood and money.
I am Big Red, tiger vicious, Big Red, bad nigger, will kill.

But there is rhythm here. Its own special substance:
I hear Billie sing, no good man, and dig Prez, wearing
     the Zoot
suit of life, the pork-pie hat tilted at the correct angle.
through the Harlem smoke of beer and whiskey, I
     understand the
mystery of the signifying monkey,
in a blue haze of inspiration, I reach for the totality
     of Being.
I am at the center of a swirl of events. War and death.
rhythm. hot women. I think life a commodity
     bargained for
across the bar in Small's.
I perceive the echoes of Bird and there is gnawing in
     the maw
of my emotions.
and then there is jail. America is the world's
     greatest jailer,
and we all in jails. Black spirits contained like
     magnificent
birds of wonder. I now understand my father urged
     on by the
ghost of Garvey,
and see a small black man standing in a corner. The
     cell, cold.
dank. The light around him vibrates. Am I crazy? But
     to under-
stand is to submit to a more perfect will, a more perfect
     order,

to understand is to surrender the imperfect self,
for a more perfect self.

Allah formed black man, I follow
and shake within the very depth of my most imperfect
    being,
and I bear witness to the Message of Allah
and I bear witness—all praise is due Allah!

                             LAWRENCE P. NEAL

CAUTION

Grandmother's raped
In the middle of the night.
Got a GOOD break.
Start out half white.

Little Black Boy, don't move too fast.
Your next step up may be your last.

Father's dead
By the white man's hand.
Welfare child
In the white man's land.

Little Black Boy, don't move too fast.
Your next step up may be your last.

Railroad's running,
Big city bound.
New way of living's
Got to be found.

Little Black Boy, don't move too fast.
Your next step up may be your last.

    Numbers, pimping,
    Bootlegging, dope,
    Trickery, guile,
    Ambition, hope.

Little Black Boy, don't move too fast.
Your next step up may be your last.

    Crime, corruption—
    Imprisonment.
    Elijah is heard—
    Enlightenment.

Little Black Boy, don't move too fast.
Your next step up may be your last.

    Hard work, devotion
    To the Muslim clan.
    Position, power—
    Elijah's Right Hand.

Little Black Boy, don't move too fast.
Your next step up may be your last.

    "Don't plead, don't beg
    To have your way.
    Non-violence is not
    The revolutionist's way."

Little Black Boy, don't move too fast.
Your next step up may be your last.

    "You're too far ahead,"
    Elijah says.
    "Be quiet, meditate,
    Mend your ways."

Little Black Boy, don't move too fast.
Your next step up may be your last.

"The Muslims have come
As far as they can.
Think I'll become
A Black Nationalist man."

Little Black Boy, don't move too fast.
Your next step up may be your last.

Known the world over—
Oratorically adept.
The world recognizes
But will not accept.

Little Black Boy, don't move too fast.
Your next step up may be your last.

Speaking, debating,
Raise freedom's shout—
Make one truth known
Before time runs out.

Little Black Boy, don't move too fast.
Your next step up may be your last.

JAMES R. LUCAS

EL-HAJJ MALIK EL-SHABAZZ

(Malcolm X)

**O masks and metamorphoses of Ahab,
Native Son**

I.
The icy evil that struck his father down
and ravished his mother into madness
trapped him in violence of a punished self
raging to break free.

As Home Boy, as Dee-troit Red,
he fled his name, became the quarry of
his own obsessed pursuit.

He conked his hair and Lindy-hopped,
zoot-suited jiver, swinging those chicks
in the hot rose and reefer glow.

His injured childhood bullied him.
He skirmished in the Upas trees
and cannibal flowers of the American Dream —

But could not hurt the enemy
powered against him there.

II.
Sometimes the dark that gave his life
its cold satanic sheen would shift
a little, and he saw himself
floodlit and eloquent;

Yet how could he, "Satan" in The Hole,
guess what the waking dream prefigured?

Then black light of partial vision came:

He fell upon his face before
a racist Allah pledged to wrest him from
the hellward-dipping hands of Calvin's Christ —

To free him and his kind
from Yakub's white-faced treachery.
He rose redeemed from all but prideful anger,

Though adulterate attars could
not cleanse him of the odors of the pit.

III.
Asalam alaikum!

He X'd his name, became his people's anger,
exhorted them to vengeance for their past;
rebuked, admonished them,

Their scourger who
would shame them, drive them
from the lush ice gardens of their servitude.

Asalam alaikum!

Rejecting Ahab, he was of Ahab's tribe.
"Strike through the mask!"

IV.
Time. "The martyr's time," he said.
Time and the karate killer,
knifer, gunman. Time that brought
ironic trophies as his faith

Twined sparking round the bole,

the fruit of neo-Islam.
"The martyr's time."

But first, the ebb time pilgrimage
toward revelation, Hejira to
his final metamorphosis:

Labbayk! Labbayk!

He fell upon his face before
Allah the raceless in whose blazing Oneness all

Were one. He rose renewed, renamed, became
much more than there was time for him to be.

                                    ROBERT HAYDEN

The Death

ONE YEAR AGO

Again he strode forward
And they waited
Escaping the grapes
The needle
The lies
For moments of hope
They knew
His heart filled with song
But he was not a
Singer
But more a choir
Of Truth
And some unfriendly
Victimized
Arose
Noise! Destruction! Hell!
But even while
Crying
They were glad
He didn't
Die
Big Red

DAVID LLORENS
(February, 1966)

MORNING RAGA FOR MALCOLM

I

O Allah . . . receive him, a morning god
bursting springly in ascendant
colors of the sun—a crescent sword slices
the shrill morning raga; in the place
of his hajih the voice tears at blood
streaked faces. dispossessed eyes flash at
the truth brillantly black.
a gnawing, pounding skin ripping voice
that does not back down—O Allah, great Spirit One
receive the gritting teeth, the bursting balls,

mangled bodies, ripped out guts spewed from piss pot
to armchair deaths. . . .
receive the unfulfilled, the unavenged; these hordes.
one expanded nigger face explodes in time, screaming
ghostly scorching everything in sight—Great Spirit One

II

I awake to see my ears and arms flying into space
to feel my legs violently crack as I stretch
for another planet: blue free voice. see free voices
    spin bluely.
spin bluely spin. spin blood hopes spin. spin resurrected
    god.

I now calm airly float
lift my spirit—Allah you
am me. space undulates.
under me, space, to my sides
and under me nothing
I now calm airly float.

LAWRENCE P. NEAL

FOR MALCOLM

Oh beautiful, black martyr
Cut down by guns held in black hands,
You and they, proclaiming the worth of being black,
But they, somehow deaf to tones of truth
Issuing from your golden black throat,
Feared for their song of hate
And in jealousy borne for your mingled melodies
    Of brotherhood, black brotherhood
    And strength, violent if need be
    With pride of real negritude,
Cut you down.

Were you to be the leader
Of a new flock from the dark skinned nation,
The mastermind of precisioned flight
Long grounded by fledglings
Grovelling in shadows of white fathers?

You were the brilliant embodiment
Of elusive manhood. Those who are less
Negate your death and fail to acknowledge
Righteousness felt of your logic.

Oh beautiful, black martyr
Cut down by black hands,
Held down by little white minds,
Send back your song to a century wrong
Yet seeking one of your golden throat
Your growing notes of truth.

JOYCE WHITSITT

IT WAS A FUNKY DEAL

It was a funky deal.
The only thing real was red,
Red blood around his red, red beard.

It was a funky deal.

In the beginning was the word,
And in the end the deed.
Judas did it to Jesus
For the same Herd. Same reason.
You made them mad, Malcolm. Same reason.

It was a funky deal.

You rocked too many boats, man.
Pulled too many coats, man.
Saw through the jive.
You reached the wild guys
Like me. You and Bird. (And that
Lil LeRoi cat.)

It was a funky deal.

ETHERIDGE KNIGHT

BROTHER FREEDOM

Lay him down gently, lay him down slow.
Swathe him in linen, wrap him just so.
Turn his young face toward Mecca's soft glow.
Our fallen warrior, our Brother Freedom.

I never met the man in person.
I only saw him once or twice.
But there was something about Malcolm
That was sincere, decent, nice. Brother Freedom.

I for one did not agree
With all the things he said,
But I defend his right to speak out
Without paying the price he paid. Brother Freedom.

They killed our Brother Freedom.
They sealed his flashing eyes.
They stilled his trumpet voice.
They smeared his soul with lies. Brother Freedom.

Judas guns snuffed out his promise,
Laid prone and silent the brilliant young hope.
Cut down for the moment the shining black manhood,
Yet did not touch a hair of Malcolm. Brother Freedom.

Immortal now, he sits in fine company
With L'Ouverture and Joseph Cinque
With Vesey, Turner and Prosser
Lumumba and Evers and others. Brother Freedom.

Brother Freedom is dead. Brother Freedom lives.
His is a spirit that swirls around us
In the vital air, inspiring all
Who seek, salute Freedom. Brother Freedom.

                                    MARGARET BURROUGHS

TO MALCOLM X

You opened our eyes, you taught us to see
the beauty of blackness, of black unity.

There was so much to do, and so little time,
shot in cold blood, while still in your prime.

Slandered and cursed, so few understood
that you were our symbol — of black manhood.

You died like the Savior, who died on the cross,
a martyr, a prophet, your black brothers' loss.

Sleep gently, black knight, we'll remember you when
you walked on this earth, black giant among men.

                                        GEORGE NORMAN

SLEEP BITTER, BROTHER

Lie craving, brother; I shall dream you peace.
Fall yearning down, my hopes shall compass yours.
Be done still seeking, you will share my search.
Keep fingers crossed when you give up the ghost,
And strings attached; there's work for ghosts to do.
Sleep bitter, brother, and at last provide
Uneasy dust beneath a restless sod.
                                        JAMES WORLEY

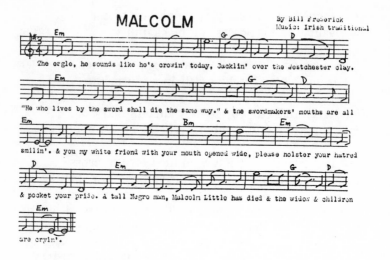

MALCOLM

By Bill Frederick
Music: Irish traditional

The eagle, he sounds like he's crowin' today, Cacklin' over the Westchester clay.

"He who lives by the sword shall die the same way." & the swordmakers' mouths are all

smilin'. & you my white friend with your mouth opened wide, please holster your hatred

& pocket your pride. A tall Negro man, Malcolm Little has died & the widow & children

are cryin'.

From the dark ghetto dens where the dope-pushers swarm
To the cold-turkey cell on the state prison farm
Bad booze & bad women & burglar alarms, & his only real friend
was a needle.

A life that's so empty you fill it with wine
A hollow heart echoes the sound of the times
In a land that is rich & a land that is fine where only a white
boy can make it.

He started to wonder & listen & learn
How white men will sizzle & crackle & burn.
The wages of misery white men will earn in the words of the
prophet Muhammed.

He joined the Black Muslims and preached for the faith
Till he followed Elijah to a big iron gate.
Now this was Elijah's Chicago estate where he waits while black
people are starvin'.

Malcolm left all the black grafters behind
To travel the world & to speak his own mind.
To search for the truth & in searchin' to find that all kinds of
                      men can be brothers.
With love for the Protestant, Catholic & Jew
Love for the cops & the K.K.K. too.
But how can you love when they're shootin' at you & you have
                      both your hands tied behind you?

He read all your books & he learned the tale well
How the colonies fought & the monarchy fell.
No non-violent marches to climb Bunker Hill — King George
                      didn't hand you your freedom.
I'm up off my back & I'm up off my knee
No promises, profits or prizes for me.
No tea at the White House until we are free & I'm willin' to
                      die for my freedom.

He climbed to the rostrum that bright afternoon
To write a new lyric & sing a new tune
To shout for his freedom & never to croon, 'cause Charlie can't
                      hear when you're hummin'.
Ol' Malcolm Little is little no more
For each one you kill there will be twenty, for:
Give a black man his finger, he'll take his whole arm. & that's
                      what ol' Malcolm was sayin'.

                Repeat first verse.

TRUE BLUES FOR A DUES PAYER

As I blew the second chorus   of Old Man River
(on an old gold trumpet   loaded with black jazz)
a shy world traveling   white Englishman   pushed a
French-Moroccan newspaper   under my Afroamerican
brown eyes   there it said that you were dead   killed by a
group of black assassins of blacker Harlems in the black
night of dark deeds   as I read the second page of blues
giving news   (I think why couldn't it have been that sad
Uncle Ralph Bunche   or one of those black blue bloods
who attend the White House policy lunch?)   I stood
facing East   with wet eyes & trembling hands   under
quiet Maghreb bright night sky I didn't cry but inside
I said goodbye to my soothsayer His Hipness Malcolm X
a true dues payer!

        TED JOANS, Goulimine, Morocco, February 23, 1965

DEATH OF THE MAN
FOR MALCOLM

Black militant man
   in structured white power
   ingrown with in-group fear
Who would bring his native land
before a world court
for redress for crimes for sins
   against humanity

The White pow/pow/pow
   er structure plots a death?
of the future of man
—a blue death for the soul brother
of Nat Turner Robert Williams
   General of the Swamps

A chain a broken promise a little
   less human with each scatter
   of energy of trust of faith

So that the connection with the gods
   becomes muddled

                 CLARENCE MAJOR

DE GUSTIBUS

Think how many men have bluntly died
With the good, familiar taste of bread
Recent on their lips. Stricken at table,
Executed unexpectedly
Following a seeming sustenant meal,
Downed by a sudden gulp or hungry battle—
That chronic disrespecter of digestion—
How quickly the dis-gusting smack of death
Slipped to salute their savoring mouths
And whittle away the staff of life
With an unobtrusive blade of cold.
Then think of the bitter bread you've known.
Be glad. Better bitter, and aware,
Than savory, a) l lulled by fickle breath.

                 JAMES WORLEY

IF BLOOD IS BLACK THEN SPIRIT
NEGLECTS MY UNBORN SON

FOR MALCOLM X IN SUBSTANCE

You must remember structures beyond cotton plains
  filled
      by joes voting for godot,
        stealing the white man's thunder,
            avarice,

        Songs of silence parade your dead body
        Distracted by housemaids' bending backs
        Gold dusted, not sinned in the angry silence
        Surrounding fetid breaths and heavy sighs
        As your actor friend tells of tall trees
        Addressing that tenth talented mind
        Bowing for recognition under the sun shining
        Cameras shaping your body

You must remember that and this second whirl of
  care
      while black brothers grieve
        your unbroken Upanishads passing the white
          man's understanding of your new peace
      without hate.
          Your new love with sweet words
      articulating complete manhood,
          directly questioning the whole and famous
      words you said.
          Let my women mourn for days
      in flight.

                              CONRAD KENT RIVERS

THE SOLITUDE OF CHANGE

(after Paula Alcocer)

FOR MALCOLM

The cavity in your breast
is like a shadowed lake
where turtledoves splash echoes
in a taciturn valley.
You were the eloquent Arab
who had come back
from the temples, singing
sheets of splendor,
a beard to keep
the flint in your melancholy eyes.
Born to sadness.
The cliché of your kind.
But you were growing
to tell the debility of color.
No, not the sad pleading
the artists of leisure would infer.
You were the manifest energy
to hold against that charge.
And what there was to charge for us,
your death delays.
                        And now,
among the energetic streets,
we wait for the obvious conclusion,
the perfect fulfillment of this encounter.
Only the night and the silence
can delight us, only
the grave keening we deplore by morning.
Forgive the stupidity of our
longing for your life.
                        Some poet
may delude us that you engineered
no change in your life, but how could
you be brave in the static fulfillment of it?

Do you listen now
as we debate our judgments?
Whatever others say of you, no matter,
take this talisman to sail briefly
over whatever dark depths you discover there.
And maybe I shall choose, like you,
to cultivate this double solitude.
Oh, glacial star, so that no one
upset the perfect fulfillment of this encounter,
my heart flies toward your solitude,
concluded on the edges of love,
in anguished goodbyes.
Until one like you wakes
to dissolve our lapidary days,
we hardly know the limits of our sails.

JAY WRIGHT

LETTER FOR EL-HAJJ MALIK EL-SHABAZZ

I ponder a death at the curb and think
Of you, Malcolm, with the clenched pain
And the surge as your body drifted with its hurt
In the alcove under the cold sheet.

I think of you in the days of your verve;
Of flaws — and dust them lightly
Not meaning to blow horns at ghetto eaves,
Nor clap at urchin scrabble and the sly wits
Of eager palms proving their skills.

I brush the jaded facets marred by touting hacks
In thin peignoirs, and leave unlit the scarfed
Decades that ministered charms in kip boudoirs
With silk-and-satin craves, where venders
Of oddities billowed in a smoke dream haze.

I page a dawdling novice who became accomplished
    liege.
Paying the maelstrom's wage, you had to fall
In your first grave; disfigured, taking grace;
Poring in bookshelf corridors in a locked place —
Flourished to eloquence and new beliefs.

Fists clubbing air, I saw you hashed; your thoughts
Unsafely shaping after that, when often in the wild
Burdock patch, eyes in your boot calling the steps,
Your startled legs would bound rerouting tracks.

Grit made you lax, even as mayhem tore your dreams
To slats, and the sweet white doves made talk,
And the black hawks and brown pigeons listened
Till at last the hour struck harp, and a flock
Of errands announced you dipped in holy founts —

Baptismal, and applause, and I discerned a tightening
Brood turning to new facades; a knit of hybrids
Focusing to build, not just for naught, but how
To reason realms: that to pave ways meant sacrifice
Even as One gave all who walked Gethsemane's shade —
Thus, tenement thickets overrun each day by vultures
Picking bones, are never safe.

Unfavorable the light . . . unswerving down the blood
    path;
Then you bared your heart, you who fetched fountains
In a sieve, who wrote of glory roads in gilt;
Small wonder at the pall your turbaned death's hood
Cast, the kaftan shrouds, seven, Islam laid to keep
You comforted where words were sparrows pecking
At the hearts of those who journeyed to the catafalque.

I hear the tolling bell! Deeper than shade, farther
Than sky our heroes lie; lip-crucified, gored
By the spate-of-hatred eyes that deem unclean
The fiber and the skin—the age-old formula, a blind,
Reducing men to swine, tearing them limb from limb
In this our time — the black purge with the red wings.

Here you were schooled for change, Malcolm,
I marked you pained and saw you tomb-engraved
In Ardsley with its pediments and shrines,
It being the time for blame in the taupe dusk . . .
I hear unutterable cries in a vexed throat, a deep lament,
And note a faded, old portfolio with its sheaves
That gently wave in evening breeze, to keep alive
The dream that carries while the dreamer sleeps.
CARMIN AULD GOULBOURNE

TWO FOR MALCOLM

I

A man of courage and despair
Shot
Because
He was
Himself.

I am
In his dialectics untutored
Understood only
He was incorruptible
Inspired in knowledge bitter
    bitter
    eyeballs bloody with spikes
    O bitter
Awesome
Rare.

Please accept my tears upon your bier.

II

He was shot, you see
For we don't tolerate one
Thunder-tongued
And incorruptible;
Too puny we
We care to buy and cheat and steal
Sit vacuous in rotten empires.
ONE against
All the vile power?
MY GOD WE CAN'T HAVE A GIANT
He might show
What man can do
With open eyes. OBVIOUSLY he must die
And let the way be devious
Say it was his kin
Call wrong right war peace poverty comfort
As is our habit.

malcolm malcolm

PATRICIA

FOR MALCOLM X

All you violated ones with gentle hearts;
You violent dreamers whose cries shout heartbreak;
Whose voices echo clamors of our cool capers,
And whose black faces have hollowed pits for eyes.
All you gambling sons and hooked children and bowery
        bums
Hating white devils and black bourgeoisie,
Thumbing your noses at your burning red suns,
Gather round this coffin and mourn your dying swan.

Snow-white moslem head-dress around a dead black
        face!
Beautiful were your sand-papering words against our
        skins!
Our blood and water pour from your flowing wounds.

You have cut open our breasts and dug scalpels in our
    brains.
When and Where will another come to take your holy
    place?
Old man mumbling in his dotage, or crying child,
    unborn?

                     MARGARET WALKER

FOR MALCOLM X

The voice has gone
Out of the wilderness
Out of the carnage kingdom
Out of the mire.
And without his eloquence
We are mute
And rocks and stones break in the soul
The world winds
On its frozen axis
The dizzy oceans churn our pain.
All needed storms abate
Themselves. Moons freeze the rain.

Gone. Delivered.
So piteous there were
The stolid and the dumb
So piteous as not to mourn
So piteous, so many
The stolid and the dumb.
Gone. Delivered.
He has gone up, delivered.

His eyes were mirrors of our agony.
They are closed.
His lips were testaments of our hunger.
They are closed.
His ears were circuits for our cries.
They are closed.
His hands were petitioners against our bondage.
They are closed.
When shall such another
Pierce and sting this land?
When shall such another
Herald this land?
Gone. Delivered.

They have shut the eyes of
The father
Before the risen womb
Over the tears of the wife
They have shrived him for the tomb
They have sent death
For the father
With the swords
And with the merciless
Voices of the guns.
They have hidden the father's death in words
And god has ceased from giving them sons
Everywhere in the vacuum land.

Toussaint! Dessalines! Marcus! Patrice!
Behold this man.
Gone. Delivered.

And we are here
With his deliverers.

If the million voices could cry "treason" —
So piteous there were
The stolid and the dumb
So piteous as not to mourn
So piteous, so many
The stolid and the dumb.
Gone. Delivered.

JULIA FIELDS

FOR OUR AMERICAN COUSINS

When Wilkes Booth thundered up the aisle
of the Audubon Ballroom,
surged through the moiling throng
with his diabolical intent,
strident shouts assailed the air:
"What is it? What is happening?"
The crowd erupted like a rocket
and Wilkes Booth cried,
"Sic semper tyrannis!"

And Talmadge Hayer raised his fateful weapon,
sighted it across the flickering gas jets,
and shot Malcolm dead.

The tat-a-tat stitched a thorn into his cheek,
traced downward over the vulnerable chest,
and thudded like a spear thrust in his side.

And Abraham swayed backward
like a severed oak
blood filling his beard,
(grown since the Hajj)
choking on his diatribes,
aghast at his own demise,
mourning our loss,
dying.

And Malcolm fell backward
into history.
Life burst from him like a jet;
struck down in mid blessing,
arms raised like a cross,
expiring.

And he was borne from the theatre
on a stretcher,
already leaving us,
life slipping silently as a sigh.
"Allah be with us."
Then black mothers moaned and wept
on the curbs of Harlem
as the crepe draped catafalque
that bore his great body
grumbled by through the mourning streets.

Then our pain was made manifest
beyond enduring.
Though we could not conceive it,
we knew.
Though we could not bear it,
we stood.
"Our Black Prince, our Shining Black Prince,
Our Manhood" . . . gone.
This was our dearest price to pay,
far dearer than Abraham.

Pennies close his eyes,
the sheet is drawn over his face.
We turn to new beginnings.
Stanton intones,
"Now he belongs to the ages."

REGINALD WILSON

SOME WHITES MOURN MALCOLM, AS IF

Somebody expert, something good at managing death
Wanted him dead, and so knew at least he was a man.
Not quite yet the prophet, king, or president,
But more than just a man . . . a black man's man,

A leader some whites mourn, as if
They too were black, dead to white,
And passing on, crowded on to nothing,
Mourning themselves by mourning Malcolm.

Somebody cornered, something cornering the seven seas
Wanted his blood, and so knew thirstily at least he
      was alive.
Loitering quietly outside the darkened camp, eyeing
      the fire,
Some whites mourn Malcolm as if they too were black,

And could hear the birth cries by which Black Majesty
      possessed him.
Clumsily, just like a man, he sought to shelter a birth,
Unlike us cool pale mourners, spooked and homeless in
      the White Power's wake.
Or didn't you see the obit, Time's cover-up, "Is God
      Dead?"

So some whites mourn Malcolm as if they had lost
      their appetite
But were not dead, at least not dead to their dying-
      machine,
A rattling, sinister cannibal fact let loose in the world
As expert, as something good to gorge upon our globe,

The unholy upshot being a four-course empire, a last
      supper
Of colored others, of Malcolm Caviar, the white Kronos
      and his kids.

The Man wanted dead his black opposite, his white
    shadow
Birthing from the nothingness of "X" to what-god-
    have-you.

Thus some whites mourn Malcolm
As if they knew what only losers know:
That the makings of men, gods and all, come and go
Mysteriously, through the flesh of friends and the
    blood of enemies.

                                        EDWARD RICHER

MALCOLM

Do not speak to me of martyrdom
of men who die to be remembered
on some parish day.
I don't believe in dying
though I too shall die
and violets like castanets
will echo me.

Yet this man
this dreamer,
thick-lipped with words
will never speak again
and in each winter
when the cold air cracks
with frost, I'll breathe
his breath and mourn
my gun-filled nights.

He was the sun that tagged
the western sky and
melted tiger-scholars
while they searched for stripes.
He said, "Fuck you white
man. we have been

curled too long. nothing
is sacred now. not your
white face nor any
land that separates
until some voices
squat with spasms."

Do not speak to me of living.
life is obscene with crowds
of white on black.
death is my pulse.
what might have been
is not for him/or me
but what could have been
floods the womb until I drown.

SONIA SANCHEZ

FOR MALCOLM X

(". . .indomitable that obelisk of a beard
    admonishes the heavens."—Malcolm Cowley.)
From my personal album
Two photos — from the news —
Hand raised by handsome chin
    toward head;
Words pouring out to resurrect the dead
Who walk among us, as Baldwin has said.

Then prostrate on a stretcher,
Eyes opened toward a sightless sky
And every passerby;
The shock as close It neared;
One remembers Sunday-school cards,
History's stoning of Stephens.
One sees — ". . . indomitable that
    obelisk of a beard admonishes the heavens."

NANINA ALBA

FLIGHT OR A WARRANT IS ISSUED FOR MALCOLM X

My relatives and friends had come
Bringing their sad faces. As usual
I was falsely accused — but no matter,
I was about to be hanged, and I
Was watched by those who had prepared me.
I did not want to die, so I feinted,
Burst the door wide, ran down the hallway,
Down the stairs and up an alley.
It felt good . . . that sweet air on my face,
My feet free beneath me.
I was very careful to cover my trail
But I could not hide my face.

So I climbed over back fences, ran down an alley
And across a sunny tennis court
Where Bernard Berenson was playing tennis
(For I had been reading him the night before)
Until I came to a gas station — and there
I was confronted by police with 38s. On my left,
The streets. On my right, a lawney hill
Which I run for, telling myself,
If they hit, they will feel like the first splash of
Sea water across your face — after that
Everything will be all right.

JOE GONCALVES

The Rage

FOR MALCOLM, A YEAR AFTER

Compose for Red a proper verse;
Adhere to foot and strict iamb;
Control the burst of angry words
Or they might boil and break the dam.
Or they might boil and overflow
And drench me, drown me, drive me mad.
So swear no oath, so shed no tear,
And sing no song blue Baptist sad.
Evoke no image, stir no flame,
And spin no yarn across the air.
Make empty anglo tea lace words—
Make them dead white and dry bone bare.

Compose a verse for Malcolm man,
And make it rime and make it prim.
The verse will die—as all men do—
But not the memory of him!
Death might come singing sweet like C,
Or knocking like the old folk say,
The moon and stars may pass away,
But not the anger of that day.

                              ETHERIDGE KNIGHT

FOR MALIK

I
Man-made lightning
    Eclipsed a black sun,
And black beetles scuttled to the wood-work
Before the
Thunder of
    instant martyrdom

II
Whilst black women,
Martyred many times before,
Moaned,
    "Lord,
We done lost our man again!"

        III
And
      Big Brother
            snorted a booger
            from his nose,
And, on cue,
A middle-class
      mid-town leader
Slobbered,
      "Amen!"

        IV
And now the beetles
      creep out
            to feed
On Malcolm's magic
      and become
Men

        V
Whilst big brother
      grinds
His brass-knuckled teeth
Behind his livid lips
      and balls his
Blood-cankered talons
      into an impotent
Angry fist
That can deal death to
Black men,
      but not to
Black Power!

                              BOBB HAMILTON

JUDGMENT DAY: FOR BIG RED,
THE DARWINIAN DOGE.
R.I.P.

Yesterday was Doomsday.
   . . . . Ask Miles —
Yesterday was Doomsday.
    And Mutants will Arise,
      Have risen.
    They infiltrate the walls of prison
Wombs . . . .
Doomsday was yesterday . . . .

Today.
    Fred Nietszche's tarbrush children,
             FAST!
        Sit gassed
    In Hyde Park cellars
Speaking in frown-invoking idioms
    Of swirling spiral nebuli
    And Aunt Samantha's sweet potato pie
          And Sartre
On many levels
    Devils they were
        Yesterday
           Was Doomsday . . . .

So Androids
    Mesmerized by T.V. sets
        Or biblical cartoons
Avoid
    Wistful regrets
        As grey baboons
    Housebroken pets . . . .

Was yesterday really Doomsday?

So Zombies
    Garbed by
Abercrombie & Fitch
        Not swift enough to scratch their
    Itching souls
        Like moles
            In a frenzy
        Burrow holes
            In quicksand . . . .

Yesterday was Doomsday
                    But
    Why scare
    The unaware
        I doubt if the Neanderthaler feared
        The hour when Cro-Magnon mind appeared.

The Oracles in tombs say:
"Yesterday was Doomsday. . . ."

                              KENT FOREMAN

THEY ARE KILLING ALL THE YOUNG MEN

Raymond A. Wood is the famous Negro N.Y.C. Police Department
infiltrator undercover agent who allegedly uncovered the "plot
to blow up the Liberty Bell and the Statue of Liberty." He is now
detective Wood.

            TO THE MEMORY AND THE ETERNAL SPIRIT
                OF MALCOLM X — 1927 - 1965

Television/radio Sunday benevolent sundown
Malcolm X assassinated
I am watching sports on network TV
and listening to WINS rock 'n roll
"Wide World Of Sports" track and field event
Negroes have long legs
& are accustomed to very yin jungle running
TV shows all
        agony of effort

athletes at once ready
they have home worked
bright bulletin precedes event
precedes contagion
        Tennessee's A&I red dog trotting team
has disappeared from the scene
and from the screen
        bulletin "Russia proclaims American Negro
                runners the best in the world."

BULLETIN
        CBS says an unidentified reporter phoned in an
                unverified report
        (THIS IS A BULLETIN!!!!)
        Malcolm X shot several times in Audubon Ballroom
                (Don't Negroes meet in the strangest places?)
WINS says Malcolm X gunned down by Negro with
        sawed off shotgun and two others and then
        returns to their gay restaurant music
        raunchy as plastic bags
then an inappropriate switch
to specialized radio
Negro Rhythm 'n Blues tune
four in a row
that as suddenly sounds like Malcolm's
funeral music
APROPOS of John Kennedy's death music
endorsed by all media of the U.S.
no jazz

no sass

Brenda Holloway soothes the Negro listening audience
with soulful hit number nine "I'll See You Again"
and with a return performance Peter, Paul & Mary
just as they sang at the stupendous March on
        Washington
sing "Blowin' in the Wind"

Kennedy's departure was vacant
unreal in the air
the FCC played strange elevator Muzak
In the hospitals the same Muzak is piped
into the rooms of critical patients
Rhythm and Blues is now
it is the reality of our Time
has Malcolm X assassinated in New York City
Dallas of the East

Incredibly
after the bulletin the TV eye carried me
to the Westminster Dog Show
sick carnivores of the dog show
officious of attendance
to THEIR dog show
under lights camera film
applause of human flippers
THE DOG SHOW OF WESTMINSTER
sick carnivores   imperious   pious
to animals they poke and pull
'the owner of THAT paranoid dog is a starlet
in an Off Broadway play'
she smiles and her teeth are blood mottled fangs
she adjusts her quivering hound
and her hands are hatchets
the bulb flashing cameras are sawed off shot guns
the announcer is an arch-angel
THE DOGS OF CARNIVOROUS WESTMINSTER
are pulled/poked into poses
of human imagination

Who says most dogs look like their masters?
as the masters discuss the most intimate details
of their pets' lives
the sex appetite   eating habits   idiosyncrasies
THE WESTMINSTER SHOW OF DOGS
the repugnance of our Time
no jazz   and   no   sass

Raymond A. Wood
the faceless Negro cop
the invisible man of New York City
and the Black Liberation Front
his photograph in the New York Post
arresting Mayor Wagner
with Herb Callender of Bronx C.O.R.E.
his brand new picture back to camera.
page one the New York Times

forty-five minutes from jail cell
forty-five minutes to dispute the F.B.I.
Forty-five minutes from rookie to detective
and the key to the City.

Ray Wood will never be heard from again
Malcolm is gone

Ray Wood back to cameras and microphones
Malcolm X chest bared to Audubon Ballroom

Assassination has become chic
destruction with terrible weapons has
become chic
to the sophisticated Establishment ipso-facto
of America
the south and the north. . .

Dallas scooped NYC with Kennedy
Los Angeles scooped the NY Police
when their soldiers gunned down seven unarmed
    Muslims
Birmingham scooped us on dogs
        (Although dogs were considered to combat
        oversized Negroes in N.Y. subways)
Inasmuch as the New York cops beat out Secretary
    of War
McNamara and the occupational force of Vietnam

with the use of poison nerve gas (Harlem riots, summer
        of 1964)
that does not count as it pertains to Foreign Policy

But the New York Press and Police Corps
in the murder of Malcolm X
have again graced themselves in the eyes
of the sophisticated men of destruction
who dress in modern uniform
indulge in modern poisons
and in florid elegance
murder

Thank you very much
for Governor George Wallace
to remind us of the North
that death to the natives (conceived in the most
        modern of offices)
has a long history
in the Nation of America
North and South   Birmingham to Harlem
        current and past
Malcolm was murdered
the day before George Washington's birthday
long weekend
            for whom?
The last long weekend for a long time
not until Easter another long weekend comes
and they could not wait
and risk a resurrection
            (they are not that inhumane)

Rank and file knowledge has the Black Muslims
infiltrated by the FBI CIA G-men Treasury agents
and the New York City Police department
who took Ray Wood out of training
to protect the Liberty Bell
and resist invaders from Canada

We have efficient Americans among us

If the Statue of Liberty was so easy to protect
    why not the life of an innocent man
        (Malcolm Little, given name)
why did not ALL the infiltrators go to their bosses
with news of the plot
Why did not J. Edgar Hoover
issue a statement that Malcolm X's life
was indeed in danger?
How much overtime pay was paid
to special secret police investigators—agitators—
    infiltrators
the weekend of Malcolm's murder?
        the long weekend
        of silent days and surmised news
was a sawed-off shotgun
missing
from the Police arsenal?
does anyone remember Patrice Lumumba?
Does anyone remember the circumstances
of HIS murder?
Is anyone concerned with the strange deaths
of bright young men
        (Kennedy, Malcolm, Lumumba, et al)

all the white faces popping up
lean with suntan oil and decay
modern uniforms
the best technological equipment
and sunglasses that adjust to the light
        (but are no good in the jungle)
This U.S. is becoming a land of 007's
from Robert Hall Clothing Stores
infiltrators from Con Edison
who pollute rivers and sky
with hot black ash
and bomb jungles
        because they cannot see in the dark

The New York Times is thin
on long weekends
the New York Post is thin
on George Washington's birthday
Their Sunday edition created Friday
their holiday-Monday edition
skeleton crew assembled
Sunday news Saturday night

The Times is thin today
yet they had someone on hand
to write Malcolm's obituary
          (or else)
they had an obituary prepared for the occasion
forty-two pages of New York Times
George Washington issue

NO JAZZ   NO SASS

D.O.A. for Malcolm
many gunshots at the Audubon Ballroom
1 cop 2 doors away
2 cops cruising
          "I got there and I saw the crowd beating a man.
          They were hysterical. So I said to my partner,
          'let's get him'. We rescued him from the crowd
          and took him into custody. Apparently he was
          badly injured. Apparently the others got away."
the cop says

Ballroom gunshots
in neutral Washington Heights
Broadway Riverside Drive Loews Rio theatre 176th St.
RKO Hamilton Palisades view and water
just below the famous Indian Museum

45 bullet shells
big guns even the anarchist will not touch

fusillade to sawed-off shot gun
Malcolm is over backwards
brothers and sisters
wooden chair clatter chorus
many shots
many arms
but we got one, the Police say
and we are hot on the trail of the others.

The thin Times today tells
of three black scrubwomen
put to work
on the blood
   (just as the handymen of Harlem were put to
   work after the riots — patching up the stores
   of the whites)
3 scrubwomen
scrubbing up blood—their blood—in time
for a Brooklyn Social Club's dance
that night
   the Audubon must go on
the New York Times marches on. . .

The alleged assassin
broken leg bullet wound and all
is rushed to Bellvue Hospital
on the opposite side of town
and one-hundred and thirty-three blocks
downtown
away from Washington Heights
away from Harlem
the Con Edison reporter
on the Daily News Television Station WPIX 11

tells us of the man 'who preached violence
   and died by his own sword'.
the man Malcolm who never was involved in violence
a pacifist until attacked

yet there are those modern men who attach
violence
　　　to 'Big Red the cocaine sniffing jailbird',
then the Con Edison reporter pauses his eulogy
to say he is glad he served Con Edison
and the Daily News station for thirteen years
and he hopes to serve them for many more
giving the evening news
Modern men of the old Confederacy

Raymond A. Wood
the faceless Negro cop
rookie spy
personally made detective
by Commissioner of Police Michael Murphy
　　　　(a man who denies his nickname is "Bull")
Raymond A. Wood back to camera
lips shut to microphones
The secret Police must go on to
higher things
Murphy smiling at the man who saved
the Statue of Liberty and the Liberty Bell
The men who murdered Malcolm X standing
a black suit back to camera
beaming Commissioner . . . a personable man
always in the Limelight
The men who murder to save us
haircut dark suit white shirt quick change from jail cell
for Wood
Faceless destruction
back to camera
assassin alleged
of Malcolm X
Hands over face
kicked and pummeled
broken leg
hands over face
invisible men
　　　　　　　　　　　DAVID HENDERSON　　winter/spring '64

BROTHER MALCOLM'S ECHO

Translated furies ring
on the page not thoughts
about life
but what should be
real people and things
loving love
this is real
the human Spirit moves
what should be
grinning molotov cocktails
replenishing the fire
WATTS happening
SHARPEVILLE burning
much too damn talking
is not
what's happening

K. WILLIAM KGOSITSILE

THE BLACK SHINING PRINCE

For you, Malcolm, where ever you are.

Big Red is
DEAD! they said as smiles from white men & the
    black bourgeois
covered his body & tomb. But he lingers on in Black
    minds. guns
        with black fingers on
        the trigger.

I
Death has taken him away. And
my heart bleeds red droplets that are black. as a
    thought. & the
darkness reminds me of his
sweet black face.
o what beauty   & gone to waste. Not
a part of this race!

II
So long are the days. And
my existence   unreal
since the departure of my   BROTHER. For
he was of my own   realm   . O
how i wish for his return   , so
far away from   home   . But

maybe it is best he stay from this cruel world today
(painted in white by insane artists in disguise.)

III
Come   death
come & rest me. introduce me
to sleep in the form
of 1000pills.LSD.WesternIdeas.Dope. In 100 doses.
    Or words in
arrows piercing my head

from the bow
of geronimo. & it need
not be formal, the introduction. "Why?" answers death,
     with the
mind of some dumb ofay.
Well,
my mind   imprisoned.
thoughts   no thoughts. not mine &
meaningless. I'd
like to experience you, my friend. Could
be better ... & maybe
               i could
               see
               Brother Malcolm

IV
Yeah. Malcolm is gone. but
he still lives on
        in the Black Masses. Betty Shabazz. LeRoi Jones.
Robert Williams. Patrice Lumumba. Black Nationalism.
&Stokely Carmichael's black power. & other people of
color in Asia, Africa & Latin America.
        & it is the reality of such people. shooting black
guns. words. insults. running through streets & alleys
screaming aloud against charlie (charley. charles. ofay.
blue-eyed. whitey) that his death will be avenged.

V
He's gone. his
death lingers on. &
so
does he.

                                    LE GRAHAM

THE DESTRUCTION OF AMERICA

After LeRoi Jones, The System of Dante's Hell.

FOR MALCOLM X LITTLE — D. 21.II.65

"I've loved about all the people I can."

& feel that love
turn to stone. boulders,
of hatred. bitterness. con-
cretions, of frozen bile. what
I've despised, when I cd still
love you, stupid mongers, killers,
blubber-headed murderers.
                                        (hate,
so fast, thru my brain,
smashing cold reservoirs
of feeling. intelligence. broken streets
of the imagination. Go,
dumb killers, keep them turned
against themselves, stolen niggers,
slaves of luxury, dead puppets
of desire, cadillacs. guns. leather
coats. the obscene repetition
of history, in politicians' bloody dreams.
power. greedheads. pimps
for the whore theyve made a-

merica (wasted land

2

make the music hard, make it
burn. to sear the ear. to

make me scream. murder silence,
don't stand for it, killers of

insane stupid dreams. move
my hands, & feet, make them work

to keep up, focus on the act of
violent music, the act

of making it. keep me away
from necks, heads, the kick

in the balls, where the feet
shd go. slitting fat throats.

the function of art, to keep
the balance. a form

so strict, so fine, it has to be,
to stay alive. ignore the blood,

fool, if you can. to keep from exploding, on the page, or in their

greedy faces. move with the
punch, with the music, against

what lies they publish,
in the rancid newspapers of the mind.

when you know, you can feel,
actually touch, the limits

of the form. white straitjackets
of emotion. the clean taste of bile,

on the tongue of love. where the mind
gives up, to the gut. guts. muscle,

bone, hard steel, of feeling. hate,
so pure, it burns. rips. tear,

claw, kick, smash their lying
backs. their "bleeding hearts."

too late, for tears. for anything,
but simple action. war. the

filthy noise, they make, when the song
runs out, to the limits

of our music. cracked lips,
bloody fingers, broken drums, play,

Musicians, play, till the racket
drowns us out. then KILL

3.

When the "form" begins to go. Crumbles. (blow, Musicians, blow)
Shattered, some lack of precision, blasted thru the end of intel-
lection. Where gut is law, the only law. Where it comes to own,
to be, what is left. What, is left us. Where we can start, now,
the shape, bent out of recognition, smeared on the page, on their
wavy faces. The Social Order, what can't be faced. What can look
like anarchy, to you, lost america, can offer you, have for you,
so much discipline, it can scare you, to death. Where the breath
runs off the page, into some silent jungle of compromise. Where
the race, has run up against it, smack, in the face. Where it can
go. "The race/ does not advance, it is only," he sd, "better pre-
served." What race, you can see. Where ever, it can go. Race.
The ends, of logic. Where what was left, is gone. Wiped out. What
song, is left to sing. Who, to sing it. (a "caucasian," with no
more use for the "race," than he had. The story, is there, in the
form. Where the "content," makes its place.Thru the forms, where
they can lead you.
                    (how to blame them, or anyone. To keep from
murdering them, in their wide-eyed sleep. What slap, to wake them.
What eyes, are theirs. Lies, they can't help, but tell. How to get
out of it. (LISTEN. What music, is left, for our ears. Where we
can take it. The forms it puts to us, for our use.

                        how to use them. how to get
                        to that point, counter-
                        point, where words move
                        into melody. song. Music,

where the sense comes dancing
thru. to feeling, the sense of
feel, how to build it, the
harmony, how the changes, the

progressions, move us, to you,
people, killers, anyone, left,
to preserve. Advance, on each
other. Dance. Sing

JOHN SINCLAIR

22. II. 65

A POEM FOR BLACK HEARTS

For Malcolm's eyes, when they broke
the face of some dumb white man. For
Malcolm's hands raised to bless us
all black and strong in his image
of ourselves, for Malcolm's words
fire darts, the victor's tireless
thrusts, words hung above the world
change as it may, he said it, and
for this he was killed, for saying,
and feeling, and being/ change, all
collected hot in his heart, For Malcolm's
heart, raising us above our filthy cities,
for his stride, and his beat, and his address
to the grey monsters of the world, For Malcolm's
pleas for your dignity, black men, for your life,
black men, for the filling of your minds

with righteousness, For all of him dead and
gone and vanished from us, and all of him which
clings to our speech black god of our time.
For all of him, and all of yourself, look up,
black man, quit stuttering and shuffling, look up,
black man, quit whining and stooping, for all of him,
For Great Malcolm a prince of the earth, let nothing
    in us rest
until we avenge ourselves for his death, stupid animals
that killed him, let us never breathe a pure breath if
we fail, and white men call us faggots till the end of
the earth.

LE ROI JONES
April, 1965

The Aftermath

MALCOLM SPOKE — who listened?
(this poem is for my consciousness too)
he didn't say
wear yr/blackness in
outer garments
& blk/slogans fr/the top 10.

he was fr a long
line of super-cools,
    doo-rag lovers &
    revolutionary pimps.
u are playing that
high-yellow game in blackface
minus the straighthair.
now
it's nappy-black
& air conditioned volkswagens
with undercover whi
te girls who studied faulkner at
smith
& are authorities on "militant"
knee/grows
selling u at jew town rates:
    niggers with wornout tongues
      three for a quarter/or will consider a trade.

the double-breasted hipster
has been replaced with a
dashiki wearing rip-off
who went to city college
majoring in physical education.

animals come in all colors.
dark meat will roast as fast as whi-te meat
especially in
the unitedstatesofamerica's
new
self-cleaning ovens.

if we don't listen.

DON L. LEE

COLOR SCHEMA

What shape has yellow? What's its sound?
Acuminate, I think, and very shrill;
For finches bobbing on my line of sight
Tug at the apex of a trailing angle
That flares a pair of whistling, glistening sides
Till definition scalds the consciousness
And they fly free.

What's purple's form and feel?
It clusters, clots, and clogs the view
With tangled damp. As months of sunmist
Drifting through the vines accumulate
In air, purples, coolly moist, condense
As grapes; we yearn; they troll us, dry,
And raisin in the sun.

And what— God feast us all— 's the taste of black?
Not bitter, as you'd think, but bland as sleep
That's just begun. I've known a bowl of black
To feed a host of most discerning men
And satisfy— at least they never sent it back
But smacked their lips and licked them; one could tell
That they fared well.

                                              JAMES WORLEY

DAYS AFTER

Mention his name and they bristle
or shake heads like steel, exhibiting
a frowned face.

Only Jesus is good enough
(although once his truth was crucified.)
Now instead of trees for crosses
their minds are melted for bullets.

This time there is no violence of
the blackened sun—surely a sign
that what has been done found favor.

"Malcolm is dead.
Amen, so be it."

          think   hope/they
          they   hope/think
          hope   think/they

On the silent eve of history's grief
Rejection whirs sedately in the air
above Cadillacs, brickhouses, community pools
and the world's most well-dressed Negro fools.
                                        HELEN QUIGLESS
                                        July, 1966

LOOK HOMEWARD, MALCOLM

Here beneath a place of comfort
Time warms the blood of some dead seeker
In waste: neither white nor African
Though still to death and far rainbows
While black youth kicks a football
Dreaming of his power vested in Americana.
With raw knowledge owing its impetus
To Malcolm, light of bearers extending
Darkness until civil rights strain for truth:
Violence weaves a carpet suggesting James Meredith
To speak against an empty assignment anti-fear.
Black faces balk, power prunes
Flowers of deep dark kept bull fights
Stirring grass rooted souls to curse peace,
Yea, cling to trouble more for more,
Body for body or reach perpetually toward Ali
Before death kicks property values through
The glass bottom constitution written like mardi gras
Postcards, in this swirling universe
Of time busting sorrow.

He remembers Betty dressing the kids,
And Alex pushing for words against time.

Even then bullets meant auralessness
Since the nigger seeds died outside a womb.
Men take power, mix their blood with dreams,
Cancel out the cancer, sunflowers and all tenses
Written in primers edited by cultureless fools
Crying in the night for higher stocks and more equity:
still the point of one less black life is not to know
or estimate how much one skin can kill enemies
though baited and dead and mouth silent
in spite of scars half-opened, words half-said,
yet even from a grave men take power and land:
men kill to live or grow wiser by trying revolutions
baked black by blood, though full of children knowing
tomorrow past their own time and place, futureless.

CONRAD KENT RIVERS
1966

MALCOLM EXSICCATED

No sooner than I heard them holler out in Harlem,
The well is dry, did I crave a drink from it . . .
I remember I used to spurn it when it brimmed—
pointing out how rife it was with impurities,
choosing the well-distilled—and dearer—libations.
I waited for it to settle, which it seemed to be doing,
gradually becoming much clearer and more enticing.
Frankly impressed that it refreshed so many others,
I often approached a pail that passed before me,
poised a dipper to take a draught, then put it off.
I hesitated too long: the source has died.
Was it really the oasis they said it was?
Though I thought not, now I will never know.
Perhaps a mere sip might have been something to
    savor. . .
Now, with fancied unquenchable thirst, afire with the
    regrets
of an inferno-fated spectre, I creep to the wall of the well
and peer into its pitch-black depth at a desert;
sand stopples my throat, and froth unparts my lips.

THEODORE HORNE

LET "X" BE HOPE

In a geometry of pain
What theorem holds, what answer heals?
Only carbon and its compounds,
Black stain running through the stone,
Endure. Words disintegrate,
And yearnings are forever swerved
By torpid hearts and careless skies.

Impaled upon satiety,
The favored alm the begging man;
While under fists of hydrogen,
Lovers and losers— scholars— fend,
Footnoting each his page of pangs:
Need is camouflaged by plight;
Who seek the wheat must brook the chaff.

This life, nothing but becoming,
Withering when it's defined,
Makes fossils of all faithlessness.
Can they that in desire would question
To the very pit of time,
From a chemistry of grief
Distill a measure of belief?

JAMES WORLEY

AT THAT MOMENT

When they shot Malcolm Little down
On the stage of the Audubon Ballroom,
When his life ran out through bullet holes
(Like the people running out when the murder began)
His blood soaked the floor
One drop found a crack through the stark
Pounding thunder—slipped under the stage and began
Its journey: burrowed through concrete into the cellar,
Dropped down darkness, exploding like quicksilver
Pellets of light, panicking rats, paralyzing cockroaches—
Tunneled through rubble and wrecks of foundations,
The rocks that buttress the bowels of the city, flowed
Into pipes and powerlines, the mains and cables of
    the city:
A thousand fiery seeds.

At that moment,
Those who drank water where he entered. . .
Those who cooked food where he passed. . .
Those who burned light while he listened. . .
Those who were talking as he went, knew he was water
Running out of faucets, gas running out of jets, power
Running out of sockets, meaning running along taut
    wires—
To the hungers of their living. It was said
Whole slums of clotted Harlem plumbing groaned
And sundered free that day, and disconnected gas
    and light
Went on and on and on. . .
They rushed his riddled body on a stretcher
To the hospital. But the police were too late.
It had already happened.

                              RAYMOND PATTERSON

THERE'S FIRE

(FOR FEBRUARY 21)

Wonder why is it I still smell smoke? . . .
I don't mean that odor of cinders
issuing from so many blockheads' tempers,
or that parched and pungent fume of eggheads
and fatheads scrambled together—and neglected.
Nor is it that stench of black and white
passions ignited in a long hot summer—
It is another sort of smoke—but not
that of burning churches in Alabama,
burning blackflesh way out in a wheatfield,
burning whitepine crosses in a frontyard,
or burning midtown mosques; it isn't quite
that kind of smoke which just now smarts
my eyes to tears, and smites my nose.
What I smell is not unlike an incense
yet stronger, stranger, and intoxicating.
I knew a source of this aroma once,
but that was snuffed out. He is cold. . .
But how is it that I still smell that smoke?
I'm hoping where there's smoke—you know the saying.

THEODORE HORNE

WHEN YOU DIED

When you died, Malcolm,
Defending and speaking
For the brother that
You loved, we mourned
Your loss.
They silenced you
With shots,
But your voice
Is heard
In other youth
Who have taken up
The fight
For Freedom.

Your ringing voice
Has filled the youth
With wild desires to speak,
And from their throats
Loud and clear,
Defiant and strong,
Have come soul stirrings
For Rights, for Freedoms, for Justice
Denied us
For so long, so long, so long.

You did not die in vain,
For the Freedoms you spoke of
WILL be won.
Though aggressive wars
WILL be fought,

Young men's blood
WILL stain the ground,
Anguished cries WILL rend the air,
Yet babies, victims of man's
Inhumanity and barbarism,
Will one day
Breathe the sweet pure air
Of FREEDOM.

CHRISTINE C. JOHNSON

WRITTEN AFTER THINKING OF MALCOLM

And if it wasn't for
All of this pressure
Perhaps, too, my art
Would be as pearls
And my songs more subtle.

But now I only know
This crude stone
In a road
Made rough with hate.

And my best song is
A beat of drums
And a shout.

ZACK GILBERT

STILLBORN POLLEN FALLING

Malik's flowers fade
among the weeds (too many
winds disperse his seeds,
robbing them of april rain,
crowding them in a cerement,
choking off another generation).

O our tomorrow poets:
stillborn pollen falling
s i l e n t l y
at the feet of our dead
& exiled poets. Wait!
The waters are rising
& the ritual begins again.

                                          EDWARD S. SPRIGGS

FOR BROTHER MALCOLM

there is no memorial site
in harlem
save the one we are building
in the street of
our young minds
till our hands & eyes
have strength to mould
the concrete beneath our feet

                                          EDWARD S. SPRIGGS

THE SUN CAME

The Sun came, Miss Brooks,—
After all the night years.
He came spitting fire from his lips.
And we flipped—We goofed the whole thing.
It looks like our ears were not equipped
For the fierce hammering.

And now the Sun has gone, has bled red,
Weeping behind the hills.
Again the night year shadows form.
But beneath the placid faces a storm rages.
The rays of Red have pierced the deep, have struck
The core. We cannot sleep.
The shadows sing: Malcolm, Malcolm, Malcolm.

The darkness ain't like before.
The Sun came, Miss Brooks.
And we goofed the whole thing.
I think.
(Though ain't no vision visited my cell).

                                    ETHERIDGE KNIGHT

BERKELEY'S BLUE BLACK

is a slender chick
running drunkenly
from her "nigger" mother
taking hours to tell
of her blackness
cannot do anything about it
except wait for the second coming
of MALCOLM
while listening to brahms or bach
until he comes

                                    EDWARD S. SPRIGGS

NO TOMB IN ARLINGTON

No tomb in Arlington
Shall hold this soldier's "rest" . . .
Proclaim, This martyr
By assassins dead. . . .
No classic "torch eternal" tell,
With sponsored breath,
His out-of-stepward quest
(Fretting as arc-weld glows
The tortured night)
Escaped from stone-hung
Crucible of death. . .
From steel-barred sanctuary,
The "Pilgrims Progress" shows,
As whores in anguish cry:

"His words incite to riot,"
To damn the Man-Child
Of the dark ghettos. . . .

Young soldier! . . .
Catalyst of commonweal. . .
Calm fountain of this
Restless, probing flame,
Bite, melt, consume crass
Citadels of dross.
Reshape, and seal a creed
With new-found name.
Dark visage turn to Meccas
From the blight.
Assault white blinding fog
With reason's light.
Emboss the face of man with
Mankind's need. . .
With flame-winged torch ignite
The myths, that succor sacred
Greed. . .
Etch deep the "vision proud"—
Your ceaseless quest,
To fuse our hopes and wills
Within the crimsoned, final gift—
The late behest,
Throbbing too deeply in the
Heart's resolve, to ever rest. . .

OLIVER LaGRONE

БАЛЛАДА О НЕИЗВЕСТНОСТИ

Посвящаю МАЛЬКОЛЬМУ ИКС
— негритянскому лидеру Органи-
зации Афро-Американского единства, погибшему 21 февр. 1965 г.
от руки убийцы.

*"...Никто из американских негров
на самом деле не знает, кто он
такой. Мы получали фамилии хо-
зяев, у которых были в рабстве."*
        МАЛЬКОЛЬМ Х

Мой прадед был простым рабом
и пропитание горбом
себе он добывал.
Мой прадед ростом был гигант;
когда пришел с войсками Грант,
раб волонтером стал.

И звали его ИКС,
как звали ИКС тебя, МАЛЬКОЛЬМ!
Сам о себе, как ты,
не знал он ничего.
Отец был ИКС, и дед был ИКС,
и предки дальние его.

Он ненавидел рабский Юг
и от рожденья однорук,
когда врагу пришел каюк
он радовался так...
Но выстрелом из-за угла
надежда ранена была
и, как подросток, умерла
у негра на руках...

И звали его ИКС,
как звали ИКС тебя, Малькольм!
Сам о себе, как ты,
не знал он ничего.
Отец был ИКС, и дед был ИКС,
и предки дальние его...

BALLAD TO THE ANONYMOUS

Dedicated to Malcolm X, Negro leader of the Afro-American
Unity Organization murdered on the 21st of February, 1965

> "None of the American Negroes actually
> know who they are. We were given the
> names of owners who held us slaves."
>   MALCOLM X

My grand-grand-dad was a common slave.
To earn his daily bread he gave
Away his sweat and tears.
My grand-grand-dad was big and strong.
When Grant and his army came along
He joined the volunteers.

His name was simply X,
Malcolm, just like yours,
And just like you, he did not know
His origin, of course.
His dad was X, his grand-dad too,
And all his ancestors.

From birth he was one-handed,
Yet fought the Southern bandits.
And when they were disbanded
My grand-grand-dad was glad.
But then a traitor hired
From round a corner fired
And budding Hope expired
In the arms of the Negro lad.

Whose name was simply X,
Malcolm, just like yours,
And just like you, he didn't know
His origin, of course.
His dad was X, his grand-dad too,
And all his ancestors.

Добавить остается мне:
родился я в иной стране,
где вот уже полсотни лет,
как слово ИКС сошло на нет.
Там равноправия рассвет,
там нет вражды
и страха нет.

Как хочешь ето назови.
Хочу, чтобы ты знал,
что у меня течет в крови
Интернационал.

Ты для других боролся, жил
и потому, Малькольм,
ты стал бессмертен,
               как Джо Хилл
и Авраам Линкольн.
Сраженный пулей ты вставал,
как символ боевой,
смеялся и друзям кивал
горячей головой...
Народ расистам вопреки
таких, как ты, родит.
Поверить могут лишь враги,
Малькольм,
              что ты убит!

Заря окрасит небосклон
над миром поутру
и вспыхнет именем: Малькольм,
как знамя на ветру.
Пусть зазвучат отныне,
как колокольный звон,
единства позывные:
Малькольм!
         Малькольм!
            Малькольм!

       ДЖЕМС ПАТТЕРСОН

Now this is what I'll add.
I, too, am a Negro lad,
But born in another land
Where names like X are banned,
Where Right and Justice reign,
And neither fear nor hate
Remain.

One more thing still remains
For me to tell you, pal.
I carry in my veins
The International.

You lived and fought for others:
All men became your brothers,
So, Malcolm, now your name
Has won immortal fame
Like Lincoln's and Joe Hill's.
Such men no bullet kills.
You fell and rose once more.
A symbol of holy war.

To friends you smile and wave
Your head, so hot and brave.
The racist bands to grieve
Your like the people bred.
Only enemies can believe,
Malcolm, that you are dead.

The dawn will light the sky,
Awakening the world
And there your name will fly
Like a flag by wind unfurled.
Let Malcolm's name from now
Sound like a clarion call
For liberty, for peace
And brotherhood for all!

JAMES PATTERSON

MEMORIAL DAY

They killed me,
Or so they thought —
That darkie is done for
They said —
And they thought
That you would not
Know me,
O h h h Mother
How they tried to
Disguise me,
To make twins
Of me and nothingness;
They dragged and trampled me
And ooooh Mother. . .
They blasted me
To a bloody black rag. . .
But I went on living,
Pumping my mangled heart
In time to
A proud and ancient past.
In time
To a proud and
Ancient past
That was ours and mine
Before this long running
Unwaking nightmare
Swallowed me
As an angry bear
Swallows a purple plum
Down into its
Ravening maw
And I went on living!
Then they flung me
Into the moiling mud
Of this backwoods stream,
Though I went on living,

For I was their
Bloodied wastecloth
That they had to
Hide away
Against the chance
Of its being seen
By some
Lonesome, honest man,
While I went on living!
And I was screaming
In the high-pitched timbre
Of a terrified rabbit,
And because men
Will to believe
That rabbits expire
Soundlessly in the
Slavering jaws
Of the hound
Only one
Or two
Heard me.
And those that heard me
Feared hounds
More than they loved humanity
As I went on living!
And I was
All at once
A big brooding sanguine eye
That saw
Hound and hunter
Skulk back
To their lairs
Yet I went on living.
And as they
Went I saw them exchange
Limbs and manners
Back and forth
So that brute-like man
Became man-like brute

Still I went on living.
And their beastish bellows
Short-shrifted
My anguished cries,
But I went on living.
And now
    they think
        all is forgot
Whilst they share
Shifty eyes
And shadowed souls,
And tell it abroad
That I never was!
But I shall go on living,
Still I shall go on living!

                              BOBB HAMILTON

NANINA ALBA

MARCELLA CAINE

MARGARET BURROUGHS

MARGARET DANNER

GWENDOLYN BROOKS

(Photo: Courtesy Johnson Publishing Co.)

THEODORE HORNE

JULIA FIELDS

MARI EVANS

BILL FREDERICK

ZACK GILBERT

LE GRAHAM

CARMIN A. GOULBOURNE

BOBB HAMILTON

RUBY DEE AND OSSIE DAVIS

CHRISTINE JOHNSON   K. WILLIAM KGOSITSILE

TED JOANS   ETHERIDGE KNIGHT

ROBERT HAYDEN

OLIVER LAGRONE

JAMES ROWSER LUCAS

DAVID LLORENS

CLARENCE MAJOR

JAMES PATTERSON

PATRICIA

RAYMOND PATTERSON

HELEN QUIGLESS

LEROI JONES

DUDLEY RANDALL

CONRAD KENT RIVERS

EDWARD RICHER

SONIA SANCHEZ

JOHN SINCLAIR

JOYCE WHITSITT

EDWARD SPRIGGS

REGINALD WILSON

BIOGRAPHICAL NOTES

NANINA ALBA is an instructor of English at Tuskegee Institute, Alabama. She was born in Montgomery, Alabama, November 21, 1917. She attended Haines Institute in Augusta, Georgia, earned an A.B. degree in 1935 at Knoxville College, and has done graduate work at Indiana University.

PUBLICATIONS: poems in *Phylon, Negro Digest, Peninsula Poets, Message Magazine, Commercial Appeal Yearbook, CEA Bulletin,* and other periodicals. Books of poetry: *The Parchments,* Merchants Press, 1963. Numerous publications in professional magazines and anthologies.

WORK IN PROGRESS: two volumes of poetry, one for fall and another for spring; short story writing continued; an anthology of campus poetry.

SIDELIGHTS: Mrs. Alba has won the Ester R. Beer Memorial Poetry Prize (second place) of the National Writers' Club. "I long for the day when our fine literary efforts are relieved of the onus of being neglected by that 'other literati.' "

GWENDOLYN BROOKS, who received the Pulitzer Prize for her volume *Annie Allen,* was born in Topeka, Kansas, June 7, 1917, and educated in Chicago. She has won a *Mademoiselle* Award for Women of the Year, an American Academy of Letters Award, and two Guggenheim Fellowships. She teaches creative writing at a junior college in Chicago, where she lives with her husband, Henry Blakely, and a son and a daughter.

PUBLICATIONS: poems in *The Negro Quarterly, Poetry, Common Ground, Harper's, Negro Digest;* in the anthologies *Poetry of the Negro, Beyond the Blues, American Negro Poetry.* Books of poetry: *A Street in Bronzeville,* New York, Harper, 1945; *Annie Allen,* Harper, 1949; *The Bean Eaters,* Harper, 1961; *Selected Poems,* Harper, 1963. She has also published *Bronzeville Boys and Girls* (for children) and *Maud Martha,* a novel. Her poem "We Real Cool" was reprinted in the Broadside Press *Broadside Series,* 1966.

WORK IN PROGRESS: she is writing a long narrative poem.

SIDELIGHTS: her novel *Maud Martha* will be reprinted in paperback by Popular Library in 1967.

MARGARET BURROUGHS, co-editor of *For Malcolm,* was born in St. Rose Parish, Louisiana, November 1, 1917. She graduated from Englewood High School, Chicago in 1933, received a B.A.E. from Chicago Teachers College in 1937 and an M.A.E.

from the Art Institute of Chicago in 1948. She has done advanced study at Teachers' College of Columbia University and at Esmerelda Institute of Art in Mexico City. She is a high school teacher of art in Chicago.

PUBLICATIONS: a poem in *Child Life;* articles in *Chicago Schools Journal; Negro Digest; Elementary English Journal; New York Public Schools; Elementary Art; Child Life; Soviet Woman* (Russia). Books (children's): *Jaycee the Drummin' Boy,* New York, Viking, 1947; *Did You Feed My Cow?,* New York, Crowell, 1955; *Whip Me Whop Me Pudding,* Chicago, Praga Press, 1966.

WORK IN PROGRESS: various articles.

SIDELIGHTS: founder: the South Side Community Art Center, Chicago; the Museum of Afro-American History, Chicago; director: State of Illinois Emancipation Centennial Exhibit, 1963; Chicago Crusader, Negro History Hall of Fame 1959, 1960, 1961; founder and director: the Lake Meadows Annual Outdoor Art Fair. She visited Europe and the Soviet Union in 1965, and the next summer led a delegation of Afro-American artists on a tour of the Soviet Union. "Special Interest: the betterment of life for all mankind and especially my people. My credo: 'Man's dearest possession is life and as it is given him to live but once, he must so live as to feel no searing regrets for years without purpose, so live that dying he might say, All my life and all my strength I gave to the finest cause in the world, the fight for the liberation of mankind.'—V. I. Lenin."

MARCELLA B. CAINE was born in Stanford, Montana, June 28, 1915. She attended Montana State University and Kinman Business College. She has been a secretary, and is now in real estate rentals. A member of Vi Gale's Workshop on Creative Writing, she has won a prize for her haiku. She is married, has two married children, and seven grandsons.

PUBLICATIONS: poems in *Negro Digest, Negro History Bulletin, Driftwood, Oregonian, Human Voice Quarterly, Cyclotron, The Saint, Cardinal Poetry Quarterly, Muse, Down Ink Lane, Jean's Journal, Poetry Dial, Green World, Karyn, Phylis, Angels, Haiku Highlights,* and in *American Women Poets* (India).

WORK IN PROGRESS: various poems.

MARGARET DANNER was born in Chicago and educated at Roosevelt College and Loyola University. She has been assistant editor of *Poetry,* has won a John Hay Whitney Fellowship, and has been Poet-in-Residence at Wayne State University. In 1959 she came to Detroit, and later founded Boone House, a center for the arts, where a group of poets including Gloria Davis, Oliver LaGrone, Edward Simpkins, Alma Parks, Harold

Lawrence, Naomi Madgett, Dudley Randall, Betty Ford, and Joyce Whitsitt met and gave poetry readings.

PUBLICATIONS: poems in *Poetry, Voices, Chicago Magazine, Negro Digest, Negro History Bulletin;* and in the anthologies *Midwestern Writers Prize Anthology; Beyond the Blues; American Negro Poetry; New Negro Poets: USA; Poets of Today,* editor Walter Lowenfels, New York, International Publishers, 1964; *Ik Ben de Nieuwe Neger; La Poesie Negro-Americaine.* Books of Poetry: *Impressions of African Art Forms in the Poetry of Margaret Danner,* Detroit, 1961; *To Flower,* Nashville, Hemphill Press, 1963; *Poem Counterpoem,* (with Dudley Randall), Detroit, Broadside Press, 1966.

SIDELIGHTS: In 1966 she visited Paris and the World Festival of Negro Arts in Dakar, Senegal. In private life she is Mrs. Otto Cunningham, and now lives in Chicago.

OSSIE DAVIS, who contributed the preface and "Eulogy of Malcolm X" to *For Malcolm,* is an actor and a playwright. He was born in Cogsdell, Georgia, December 18, 1917. He has acted in Broadway productions in 1946, 1950, 1957, 1959, and in 1962 he played the title role in his own three-act comedy, *Purlie Victorious.* He played in the motion picture *The Cardinal* in 1963. His wife is the actress, Ruby Dee.

PUBLICATIONS: *Purlie Victorious,* New York, French, 1961.

MARI EVANS was born in Toledo, Ohio . . . attended the University of Toledo . . . divorced, has two sons . . . has worked variously as a musician, choir director, church organist, and director of adult program promotion at the Indianapolis Fall Creek Parkway YMCA . . . Associate Editor of an industrial magazine for the past three years . . . currently responsible for publications at Atterbury Job Corps Center. Member Indiana Industrial Editors' Association . . . made honorary John Hay Whitney Fellow, 1965-66.

PUBLICATIONS: poems in *Dialog, Negro Digest, Phylon;* and in the anthologies *New Negro Poets: USA,* Langston Hughes; *American Negro Poetry,* Arna Bontemps; *Poets of Today,* Walter Lowenfels; *Schwarzer Orpheus,* Janheinz Jahn, *Beyond the Blues,* Rosey Pool; *Ik Ben de Nieuwe Neger,* Rosey Pool; *Black America,* Sveriges Radio; *People in Poetry,* Gateway English Series; *Lena,* Horne and Schickel; *Negro Humor,* Langston Hughes.

SIDELIGHTS: Work has been broadcast in the United States and England, used in university and college workshops, used in the 1963 Aldeburgh Poetry Festival in England, used in National Educational Television's *History of the Negro,* and in the Broadway production *A Hand Is On the Gate.*

JULIA FIELDS was born January 21, 1938 in Uniontown, Alabama. She attended Hatch High School and gained a B.S. degree from Knoxville College in 1961. She was in residence at the Breadloaf Writers Conference in Middlebury in 1962, and studied for a summer at the University of Edinburgh in Scotland. She teaches English in the public schools of New York City.

PUBLICATIONS: poems in *Negro Digest, Massachusetts Review,* and *Riverside Poetry II.* Poems in the anthologies *Beyond the Blues; New Negro Poets; USA; Ik Ben de Nieuwe Neger,* editor Rosey E. Pool, The Hague, Bert Bakker, 1965; *La Poesie Negro-Americaine;* and *American Negro Poetry,* editor Arna Bontemps, New York, Hill and Wang, 1963.

SIDELIGHTS: a three-act play, *All Day Tomorrow,* was performed by the Drama Workshop of Knoxville College in May, 1966 with proceeds going to the Alumni Fund. Two one-act plays, *A Fool in Earnest* and *An Anarchist in Exile,* will be produced by the Drama Workshop in 1966 or 1967.

KENT FOREMAN is a Chicagoan who reads his peoms in bars and coffee houses in Chicago. He directed Oscar Brown's *Summer in the City* and also took part in the writing of it.

BILL FREDERICK, a topical songwriter and singer, was born in Philadelphia, Pennsylvania, January 30, 1943. He received a B.A. from the University of Pennsylvania in 1963, and spent three years of postgraduate study there. He lives and works in Philadelphia.

PUBLICATIONS: 11 songs in *Broadside Magazine.*

WORK IN PROGRESS: "compiling songbook, and looking for a record company with guts."

SIDELIGHTS: "have sung in numerous colleges in Pennsylvania, coffeehouses in Phil. and NYC, benefit concerts, demonstrations (including March on Washington, April 1965—SDS). First saw Malcolm on TV and heard him speak at U. of P. in 1963. Later, read his speeches in *The Militant.*

"I enclose a song about Malcolm, written on the day of his funeral. I am a writer and singer of radical songs, and have tried this song on both black and white audiences, with good response . . . When Malcolm was shot, I expected dozens of songs to come out, like after the Kennedy assassination, but this is the only one I've seen . . . To be any good, a song must be a good poem."

ZACK GILBERT was born April 21, 1925 in McMullen, Missouri, and attended Sumner High School in Cairo, Illinois. He is an insurance agent and broker in Chicago.

PUBLICATIONS: poems in *Negro Story, Voices, Ebony Rhythm, Negro Digest.* In 1965 he conducted a column, "A Broader View," in the *Chicago Bulletin-Booster.*

WORK IN PROGRESS: a novel: *Way Out World of Hooks and Nails.*

SIDELIGHTS: his poem "A Tribute to JFK" will be in the Scott, Foresman and Company's *Seventh Grade Reader Anthology* (1967). His poem "Secret Prayers of Ol' Joe," translated into Dutch by Rosey Pool, is in Dr. Simons' Dutch sociological work about skin color and social conditions. The poem originally appeared in *Voices,* edited by Langston Hughes.

CARMIN AULD GOULBOURNE was born February 22, 1912 in El Cristo, Cuba and reared in Jamaica, West Indies. A homemaker and the mother of two sons, 23 and 16, she lives in the Bronx, New York. She is attending Morris Evening High School and will graduate in January 1967.

PUBLICATIONS: Poems in *Negro Digest, Chicago Jewish Forum, The Hilltop* (Howard University), the *Amsterdam News,* the *Morris Evening News* and the *Bronxdale Telstar.*

WORK IN PROGRESS: Several short stories.

SIDELIGHTS: "I came to the United States at the age of 15. Attended Public School for a year and because of poor circumstances I had to leave school to earn enough money to support myself. I have been writing for many years with a limited amount of success. Whatever I have accomplished so far, I owe to my cousin, Professor Ivan E. Taylor, who is head of the English Department at Howard University. A writer himself, he has been my constant help through the years, generously giving of his time to advise, encourage and lead me in the right channels toward greater achievement."

LE GRAHAM is a teacher of applied arts in Detroit, Michigan. He was born February 18, 1940 in Savannah, Tennessee, but he calls Oak Ridge, where he attended high school, his home town. He received a B.S. degree from Tennessee A. and I. University in 1962 and an M.S. from Stout State University, Wisconsin in 1963. He served in the Army from 1963 to 1965, the last year as an administrative assistant at the Army Education Center in Ansbach, Germany.

PUBLICATIONS: a book of poetry, *The Black Narrator.* Detroit, Harlo Press, 1966.

WORK IN PROGRESS: an autobiographical novel, Afro-American art creations, and a volume of poetry.

SIDELIGHTS: In 1963 he worked as a recreation supervisor (of a black community) in the atomic city of Oak Ridge, Tennessee. In 1965 he worked on an autobiographical novel in Amsterdam, Holland. In June, 1966 he exhibited Afro-American creations in applied arts at the first annual Black Arts Convention and Work Shop held in Detroit, Michigan. He has also written one-act plays and essays.

BOBB HAMILTON is a painter, sculptor and ceramicist as well as a poet. He was born in Cleveland, Ohio, December 16, 1928. He graduated from Ohio State University in 1950, and won a writing scholarship of the New School for Social Research in its Summer Workshop in 1957. He is an art teacher for the Welfare Department in New York City.

PUBLICATIONS: poems in *Negro Digest, Yugen, Soulbook;* and in the anthologies *Beyond the Blues* and *Mentor Book of Religious Verse,* editors Horace Gregory and Marya Zaturenska, New York, New American Library, 1956. Malcolm article in *Soulbook.*

WORK IN PROGRESS: a volume of poetry, a biography, and a script for a jazz movie.

SIDELIGHTS: "In Cleveland, Ohio, in the ghetto, where I grew up everyone said whilst [used in his poem] in spite of all that the teachers could do to 'civilize' us (smile) there are lots of other archaisms that I used until I went to college and then became self-conscious behind my degree! My neighborhood was really a southern black community moved north, and the language there was often 'quaint' so to speak. What I tried to capture in the poem was the flavor of the black storefront preacher and his female congregation. When Malik was murdered, even here in New York, the impact on the old folks was very like that of a congregation that had been whipped up about the story of the crucifixion on a Sunday morning. I remember how my granny used to get when she talked about Marcus Garvey. My use of the term [whilst] was not pretentious but an attempt to go back, so to speak to the way our people responded to an emotional shock as I remember it. Malcolm did have that kind of appeal to the older people—I've even seen them shout at some of his indoor speeches."

ROBERT HAYDEN was born in Detroit, Michigan, August 4, 1913. He attended public schools there and earned a B.A. at Wayne University and an M.A. at the University of Michigan. He has been music and drama critic for the *Michigan Chronicle,* an English instructor at the University of Michigan, and is now Associate Professor of English at Fisk University, where he teaches creative writing. He lives in Nashville with his wife and his daughter. He is a member of the Bahai faith. He won Hopwood Awards for Poetry in 1938 and 1942, and the Dakar Award in 1966. He had a Rosenwald Fellowship in Creative Writing in 1947, and in 1954 a Ford Foundation Fellowship carried him to Mexico.

PUBLICATIONS: poems in *Atlantic Monthly, Negro Digest, Poetry, Midwest Journal, Voices, Phylon, United Asia, World Order;* and in the anthologies *The Negro Caravan, Negro Poets and Their Poems, Poetry of the Negro, Beyond the Blues,* and *American Negro Poetry.* Books of poetry: *Heartshape in the Dust,* Detroit, Falcon Press, 1940; *A Ballad of Remembrance,* London, Paul Breman, Ltd., 1962; *Selected Poems,* New York, October House, 1966. Poetry pamphlets: *The Lion and the Archer,* with Myron O'Higgins, Nashville, 1948, (Counterpoise Series No. 1); *Figure of Time,* Nashville, Hemphill Press, 1955, (Counterpoise Series No. 3). His ballad "Gabriel" was reprinted in the *Broadside Series* in 1966.

WORK IN PROGRESS: poem on polar exploration; an anthology, *Kaleidoscope,* for Harcourt, Brace; and a one-act play.

DAVID HENDERSON was born in Harlem in 1942. He attended Hunter College and the New School for Social Research in New York City.

PUBLICATIONS: Poems in the *National Guardian, East Village Other, Umbra,* the *Seventh Street Quarterly,* and *The Black American;* and in the anthologies *New Negro Poets: USA,* editor Langston Hughes, Bloomington, Indiana University Press, 1964; *Poems Now,* editor Hettie Jones, New York, Kulchur Press, 1966; and in *La Poesie Negro-Americaine,* editor Langston Hughes, Paris, Editions Seghers, 1966. A book of poems, *Felix of the Silent Forest,* to appear December 1966.

WORK IN PROGRESS: He is working on a novel, a book of essays, and a book of poems tentatively entitled *Cities.*

SIDELIGHTS: His poems have appeared in a record album, *Jazz Poets,* and have been performed by the Free Southern Theater. "Some of us in New York would like to see a commission report or volumes of aspects of [Malcolm's] death *a la* Kennedy."

THEODORE R. HORNE was born October 12, 1937 in Washington, D.C. He received a B.A. at Howard University in 1958, and pursued further study at the University of Bordeaux (France) and at New York University.

PUBLICATIONS: poems in *Soulbook.*

WORK IN PROGRESS: two short plays.

SIDELIGHTS: He attended the New York City Writers' Conference in July 1964, and the First World Festival of Negro Arts (Dakar, Senegal) in April 1966.

TED JOANS "born Cairo, Illinois, July 4th, 1928, AmExCo Rotterdam Holland Northside Hi Indiana U BA Fine Arts (painter) 1950. Occupation jazz poetry surrealist paintings, and jazz music. War service war plant.

"HAVE BEEN PUBLISHED: *Presence Africaine Nouvelle Somme de Poesie du Monde Noir* 66/ *La Poesie Negro Americaine* Edition Seghers 66/ *Ik Ben de Nieuwe Neger* Holland 65/ *Poetry Is For People* Boston 65/ *Black Poets* USA NYC 64/ *New Negro Poets* Indiana 64/ *City Lights Journal* San Francisco 63/ *Negro Verse* London 63/ *Beyond the Blues,* England 62/ *Beat Scene* NYC 60/ *Jazz Dichterung* Hamburg 62/ *The Bird* NYC 63/ *The Beats* NYC 61/ *The Hipsters* (book of collages & prose by Ted Joans) Citadel Press 60/ *All of T.J. and No Mo'* poems by Ted Joans NYC 1960, 61, 62, 63, 64/ *Antologi della Beat Poetica* Milano 63/ *Funky Jazz Poems* NYC 59/ *Protest Dichter* Holland 64/ *Happenings Internationale* Amsterdam 66/ *La Breche Revue Surreallist* Paris 62, 64, 66.

"WORKS IN PROGRESS: *Spadework: an Autobiography of a Hipster* (City Lights perhaps 67?); *Niggers from Outer Space, a Black Power Novel.*

"SIDELIGHTS: The late Andre Breton the founder of surrealism said that I was the only Afro-American surrealist and welcomed me to the exclusive surrealist group in Paris. Timbuctu is my chosen place of self imposed exile and I remain there during the winter months and come to Europe to earn money each summer. Have three sons with African names Ted Nkrumah, Lars Kimani, and Tor Lumumba."

CHRISTINE C. JOHNSON is a school teacher in Chicago. She was born January 15, 1916 in Versailles, Kentucky and attended Georgetown High School. She earned a B.S. degree at Loyola University and did postgraduate work at the University of Chicago. As, a child she won a gold medal for poetry. She has been a nurse, an occupational therapist, and principal and director of the University of Islam in Chicago.

PUBLICATIONS: poems in *Cadence* and *Outlook Magazine.* A first grade reader, *Muhammad's Children,* 1963.

WORK IN PROGRESS: a second grade history.

SIDELIGHTS: she has made five trips to Africa and Europe, visiting Russia in 1960, and has also visited Asia.

LEROI JONES was born October 7, 1934, in Newark, New Jersey and attended public schools there. He received his A.B. from Howard University in 1954 and did graduate work at the New School for Social Research and Columbia University. He served in the Air Force from 1954 to 1957. He won a Whitney Fellowship in 1961-62 and a Guggenheim in 1964-65. His play *The Dutchman* received the Obie (Off Broadway) Award for 1964 as the Best American Play. *The Toilet* was cited as one of the Best Plays of 1964-65 in the anthology *Best Plays of 1964-65.* *The Slave* received honorable mention for drama in English in the Festival of Negro Arts at Dakar in 1966. He lives in Newark, N.J.

PUBLICATIONS: poems in *Liberator, Soulbook, Evergreen Review, Paris Review, Black Dialogue, Downbeat, Afro-American Magazine, Rights & Reviews, Revolution, Negro Digest, Broadside Series* (1967), other magazines; in the anthologies *Beyond the Blues,* editor Rosey E. Pool, Kent, England, Hand and Flower Press, 1962; *American Negro Poetry,* editor Arna Bontempts, New York, Hill and Wang, 1963; *New Negro Poets: USA,* editor Langston Hughes, Bloomington, Indiana University Press, 1964; and others. Books of poems are: *Preface to a Twenty Volume Suicide Note,* New York, Corinth, 1961; *The Dead Lecturer,* New York, Grove, 1964; *Black Art,* Jihad, 1966. Other books are: *Blues People,* New York, Morrow, 1961; *The Dutchman and The Slave,* Morrow, 1964; *The System of Dante's Hell,* Grove, 1965; *Home,* Morrow, 1966.

WORK IN PROGRESS: *Book of Life* (philosophy); various plays.

K. WILLIAM KGOSITSILE was self-exiled from South Africa in 1961. He was born in Johannesburg September 19, 1938 and attended Madibane High School there. In this country he has attended Lincoln University, the University of New Hampshire, and Columbia University. He is currently studying at the New School for Social Research in New York City under the sponsorship of the African-American Institute.

PUBLICATIONS: poems in *Soulbook, Negro Digest,* and *Transition* (East Africa); and in the anthology *Poems Now,* editor Hettie Jones, New York, Kulchur Press, 1966. Articles and essays in *Liberator, Tuesday, Soulbook,* etc. He has unpublished book of poems called *Mahube.*

WORK IN PROGRESS: a book of essays.

ETHERIDGE KNIGHT, who writes from Indiana State Prison, was born in Corinth, Mississippi, April 19, 1933. He has four sisters and two brothers. He has been a medical technician, and served in the U.S. Army in Korea, Guam, and Hawaii.

PUBLICATIONS: poems in *Negro Digest, The Goliards, Orphic Lutes,* and *Cardinal Poetry Quarterly.* Short stories in *Negro Digest, Jaguar, Music Journal,* and *Prison Magazine.*

WORK IN PROGRESS: a historical novel about Denmark Vesey. (He needs data, especially a map of Charleston, South Carolina about 1822.)

SIDELIGHTS: "I died in Korea from a shrapnel wound & narcotics resurrected me. I died in 1960 from a prison sentence & poetry brought me back to life . . .

"About the line: 'Compose (a verse) for Malcolm man,' No, I didn't mean for 'man' to be a vocative. Rather I meant for 'man' to be a term of endearment, an affectionate attachment to Malcolm. You know like 'ito & ita' is in Spanish? To me, 'man' & 'boy' serve the same purpose—like: Charlie boy, Sonny man, etc. Also, without the comma, the reader is less likely to make the mistake of thinking that I'm addressing him—which I am not. Further, 'man' simply for what it means literally and visually shows the inseparateness of the two, Malcolm & man.

"I was aware of what I was doing to the King's English. And that's my biggest bug. I mean—I don't think in proper English therefore my expressions (and ideas) are not in proper English. Don't get me wrong, I'm not knocking good English; in fact, when a push comes to a shove, I can handle it. But man, it limits me sometimes—like traditional meter, foot & form. I wish I knew another language. They tell me Swahili is out of sight."

OLIVER LAGRONE is a poet, and a sculptor whose work is in many collections and has been the subject of columns by Ernie Pyle and George Stark. He was born in McAlester, Oklahoma, a son of a minister, and attended Howard University and graduated from the University of New Mexico. He has done advanced study at Cranbrook and Wayne State University. He has been an international representative for the UAW-CIO, and is now a teacher in special education in the Detroit Public Schools.

PUBLICATIONS: poems in *Saturday Review, Correspondence, Negro History Bulletin,* the *New York Times, Manchester Guardian, Negro Digest, Peninsula Poets;* and in the anthologies *Beyond the Blues, New Negro Poets,* and *La Poesie Negro-Americaine.* Books of poetry: *Footfalls,* Detroit, Darel Press, 1950; *They Speak of Dawns,* Detroit, Brinkley-Leatherman, 1963.

WORK IN PROGRESS: *Fragments of a Splintered Dream,* a book of poems.

SIDELIGHTS: LaGrone's interest in Negro history and art has created a demand for his services as a lecturer and consultant in the area of Afro-American culture. As a teacher in Detroit's public schools he has been an active advocate of curriculum changes that would bring a more historically honest picture of the Negro into school texts. William Rose Benet favorable reviewed *Footfalls* for the *Saturday Review,* and a Columbia University doctoral candidate has made a study of his poetry for his Ph. D. seminar.

★

DAVID LLORENS was born in Chicago, October 12, 1939, and graduated from John Marshall High School there. He has a few semester hours of credit from several colleges. He served in the Air Force in Turkey. He has been managing editor of the *Woodlawn Booster,* a community newspaper in Chicago, assistant editor of *Negro Digest,* and at present is a free lance writer.

PUBLICATIONS: poems in *Negro Digest;* articles in *Negro Digest* and *The Black Student;* book and record reviews in *Negro Digest.*

WORK IN PROGRESS: Essays and articles on various subjects.

SIDELIGHTS: He has been a SNCC worker in Mississippi. His poem "One Year Ago," which heads the second section of this anthology, was his first attempt at writing a poem for publication.

JAMES ROWSER LUCAS'S "Caution" is his first published poem. Mr. Lucas was born January 13, 1931 in Falmouth, Virginia and attended Walker-Grant High School in Fredericksburg. He received a B.A. from Howard University in 1951. He is a postal clerk and lives with his wife and children in Baltimore.

WORK IN PROGRESS: collaboration on play based on the Frankie and Johnny story.

SIDELIGHTS: "My only other literary accomplishment has been a letter to the editor of *Life Magazine.* I do work continuously though and have reams of rejection slips to prove it. Hobbies — polaroid photography — collecting jazz recordings — reading — attending concerts."

CLARENCE MAJOR was born in Atlanta, Georgia, December 31, 1936. He served in the Air Force, and is now a welder in a steel plant in Omaha, Nebraska. He has edited *Coercion Review,* and been book-reviw editor for *Anagogic* and *Paideumic Review.*

PUBLICATIONS: his poems have appeared in many little magazines, among them *Black Orpheus, The Fiddlehead, East and West* (India), *Letras da Provincia,* (Brazil), *Camels Coming, Galley Sail, The Outsider, Umbra, Kauri, Coffin, Showcase, Graffiti, The Flys Eye, Literary Review, Entrails, Free Lance, Beatitude, Poetaster, Poetry Pendulum, Poetry Digest,* etc. He has poems in *American Negro Poetry* and *Where Is Vietnam?,* New York, Doubleday, 1966. His short stories have appeared in *Hearse* and in *Olivant Annual Anthology of Short Stories* for 1957, 1959, and 1966. His articles have appeared in *Negro Digest, Bronze Mirror,* and *Proof.*

Books of poems: *Love Poems of a Black Man,* Coercion Press, 1964; *Human Juices,* Coercion, 1965.

WORK IN PROGRESS: he is presently at work on a novel.

SIDELIGHTS: he has seven novels being circulated by two agents in New York. His article on Malcolm X appears in the December 1966 *Negro Digest.* He has also written articles on LeRoi Jones, Cleanhead Vinson, and Frank London Brown.

★

LAWRENCE P. NEAL, editor of *Pride Magazine,* was born in Atlanta, Georgia, September 5, 1937. He attended Roman Catholic High School in Philadelphia and graduated from Lincoln University, Pennsylvania in 1961, where he won Literary Prizes in 1960 and 1961. He did postgraduate study at the University of Pennsylvania..

PUBLICATIONS: poems in *Liberator, Soulbook, Black Dialogue, Negro Digest, Cheyney Review.*

WORK IN PROGRESS: a critical biography of Richard Wright and a play tentatively entitled *Black Episodes.* He is completing an anthology of Afro-American poetry and prose with LeRoi Jones, to be published by William Morrow and Sons.

SIDELIGHTS: "Formerly arts Editor of *Liberator Magazine;* am the educational director of the New York Black Panther Party. Was active in the Uptown movement in poetry along with Rolland Snellings and Willy Kgositsile and other poets who felt that the Black artist must communicate directly with his own people. I see my work as the spiritual, cultural, and political voice of my people, and I place it at their service. I feel that Black America is the final arbiter of the works of her artist. The life and death of Malik Shabazz (Malcolm X) represents a significant turning point in the history of Black America."

GEORGE E. NORMAN was born in Detroit, Michigan, December 26, 1923 and attended Prairieview College. He was a Navy musician during World War II. He has composed more than 500 songs, many of which have been published and recorded. He created a Negro history exhibit which many historians and scholars have acclaimed as one of the finest in the nation. He is a post office clerk in Detroit. He is presently working on a book of Negro history.

★

PATRICIA is the pen name of Mrs. Patricia McIlnay, who was born in Battle Creek, Michigan, March 15, 1934 and attended high school there. She graduated from Michigan State University in 1956 with a B.A. degree. She lives in New York City, where she is a teacher.

PUBLICATIONS: poems in *Freedomways*.

WORK IN PROGRESS: a volume of poetry and a prose poem.

SIDELIGHTS: "I am a correspondent for *Transmondo*, a world-wide news & photo agency based in N.Y., editor-in-chief, Marc Crawford. The agency specializes in coverage of the civil rights struggle."

★

JAMES PATTERSON was born in Moscow, Russia, in 1933. His father was an Afro-American journalist who left the United States for the Soviet Union in 1932 and became a Soviet citizen. Patterson studied at a naval institute and served as an officer in the Russian Navy. In 1956 his poems began appearing in magazines. In 1957 he entered the Gorky Literary Institute to prepare for a career as a poet. In 1963 his first book was published.

PUBLICATIONS: poems in the magazines *Ogonek, Moskva, Sovietskii Voin, Sovietskaya Ukraina*. A book of poems, *Rossiya Afrika*, 1963.

★

RAYMOND PATTERSON was born in New York in 1929, and attended Lincoln University (Pennsylvania) and New York University. As an undergraduate, he received a first prize for poetry in a competition sponsored by the University of Pennsylvania Press. He has taught English in the New York public schools and has worked as a counselor for delinquent boys. He initiated a series of poetry readings by Negro poets in New York's Market Place Gallery.

PUBLICATIONS: his poems have appeared in *Umbra* and in the anthologies *Ik Zag Hoe Zwart Ik Was; Sixes and Sevens; Beyond the Blues; Poets of Today; New Negro Poets: USA.*

HELEN G. QUIGLESS was born in Washington, D.C., July 16, 1944. She attended the Putney School in Putney, Vermont, Bard College and Fisk University, where she received an A.B. in English in 1966. She lives in Tarboro, N.C.

PUBLICATIONS: poems in *The Fisk Herald.*

SIDELIGHTS: She was in John Oliver Killens' Writers' Workshop at Fisk University and studied creative writing under Robert Hayden at Fisk and Ed Dodd of Dodd and Mead at the Putney School.

DUDLEY RANDALL, co-editor of *For Malcolm,* was born January 14, 1914 in Washington, D.C. He attended the public schools of Washington, East St. Louis, and Detroit, and graduated in 1949 from Wayne University, where he was a member of the Miles Modern Poetry Group with Robert Huff and Paul Petrie. He received a master's in library science from the University of Michigan in 1951, and is now working on a master's in humanities at Wayne State University. He has been a foundry worker in an automobile factory, a letter carrier, a post office clerk, and a librarian at Lincoln University of Missouri and Morgan State College, and is now a reference librarian in the Wayne County (Michigan) Federated Library System. During World War II he served with a Signal Corps unit in the South Pacific. He has a married daughter and lives with his wife and his nephew in Detroit.

PUBLICATIONS: poems in *Midwest Journal, Free Lance, Negro Digest, Correspondence, Umbra, Negro History Bulletin, Peninsula Poets, Beloit Poetry Journal, Wayne Review.* Poems in the anthologies *Beyond the Blues; American Negro Poetry; New Negro Poets: USA; Ik Ben de Nieuwe Neger; La Poesie Negro-Americaine; Kaleidoscope* (1967). Books of poetry; *Poem Counterpoem* (with Margaret Danner), Detroit, Broadside Press, 1966. Short stories in *Negro History Bulletin* and *Negro Digest;* articles in *Negro Digest* and professional journals; book reviews in *Midwest Journal* and *Negro Digest.*

SIDELIGHTS: he won a Tompkins Award for poetry and fiction in 1962 and another for poetry in 1966. He owes a debt of gratitude, for awakening him from dormancy, to Rosey Pool for her interest and to Margaret Danner for her "I thought you said you were a poet!" He has translated Latin, French and Russian poetry. In the summer of 1966 he visited Paris, Prague, and the Soviet Union with a delegation of Afro-American artists. His ballads *(Broadside Series)* have been set to music and recorded by folksinger Jerry Moore. In 1965 he started Broadside Press, publishing broadsides of contemporary poets. *For Malcolm* is the first book attempted by Broadside Press. In 1962-1964 he worked with Margaret Danner in her Boone House cultural center, with James Thompson, Oliver LaGrone, Naomi Madgett, and Joyce Whitsitt.

WORK IN PROGRESS: a novel and a book of poems.

EDWARD RICHER is an instructor in English and journalism at St. Cloud State College, Minnesota. He was born March 1, 1930 in Mason City, Iowa. He graduated from the University of Minnesota in 1954, and did graduate study there and at the Writers' Workshop of the State University of Iowa.

PUBLICATIONS: poems in *Minnesota Review;* articles in *Liberation, Studies on the Left,* and *Venture No. 1.*

SIDELIGHTS: "My first teaching job was in the South, at the University of Florida (Gainsville), 1961-1965. I was active in the movement less than a year when that school's vice-president (Harry Philpott, now president of Auburn!) unilaterally had me terminated for advising students to play a militant role in the local Afro-American struggle for freedom. I spent a year and a half fighting them, even tried to start a school (Free University of Florida), but eventually I was starved out. They play for keeps: liberals, moderates, and native fascists alike; people in this country who want freedom will have to learn, in their own way, how to play for keeps as well."

CONRAD KENT RIVERS was born October 15, 1933 in Atlantic City, New Jersey. He attended Wilberforce University, and now teaches English at a Gary, Indiana high school and lives in Chicago.

PUBLICATIONS: poems in *Kenyon Review, Negro Digest, Antioch Review, Free Lance;* and in the anthologies *Beyond the Blues, American Negro Poetry,* and *New Negro Poets: USA.* Books of poetry: *These Black Bodies and This Sunburnt Face,* Cleveland, Free Lance Press, 1964.

WORK IN PROGRESS: *The Still Voice of Harlem,* a book of verse.

SONIA SANCHEZ was born in Birmingham, Alabama, September 9, 1935. She earned a B.A. at Hunter College in 1955, and has taken writing courses at New York University. She is a teacher, and lives in New York with her nine-year-old daughter.

PUBLICATIONS: poems in *Transatlantic Review, Negro Digest, Liberator, Soulbook, Revolution, Minnesota Review, New England Review.*

OTHER PUBLICATIONS: *Afro-American Festival of the Arts.*

WORK IN PROGRESS: a creative writing book for teachers.

SIDELIGHTS: "Have read my poems over WRVR-FM in N.Y.C.; Have written two one act plays."

JOHN SINCLAIR is a jazz critic and editor of the Artists' Workshop Press, Detroit. He was born in Flint, Michigan, October 2, 1941, and attended high school in Davison, Michigan. He studied at Albion College and received an A.B. in 1964 from the University of Michigan Flint College. He did graduate work in 1964-65 at Wayne State University.

PUBLICATIONS: poems in *El Cornu Emplumado, Out of Sight, OR, Spero, Work, Change, Art & Artists, Jazz, It;* and in the anthology *Poems Now,* editor Hettie Jones, New York, Kulchur Press, 1966. Books of poetry: *This Is Our Music,* Detroit, Artists' Workshop Press, 1965; *The Leni Poems,* Artists' Workshop Press—Grist Press, 1966; *Bridgework,* Fenian Head Centre Press, 1967; and *Fire Music: a Record,* Artists' Workshop Press, 1966. Record reviews and articles in *Downbeat, Jazz, Coda, Sounds & Fury.* Book reviews in *Kulchur, New University Thought, Work, Whe're.*

WORK IN PROGRESS: *Corrections: a Book of Law.*

SIDELIGHTS: "Editor & publisher of Artists' Workshop Press; editor *Work* (poetry), *Change* (new/jazz magazine), *Whe're* (literary magazine) . . . The third section (of poem) should appear just as it is, i.e. it looks like prose but the line breaks, even in that mess, make their own sense . . . And you can add this note, if you have a 'notes on contributors' section, that 'like Archie Shepp said about his music, *all* my work is for Malcolm.' "

EDWARD S. SPRIGGS is East Coast editor of *Black Dialogue.* He was born December 6, 1934, in Cleveland, Ohio, and educated at George Washington High School in San Francisco and at San Francisco State College, where he received his B.A. in 1965. He is a graphic artist and painter as well as a poet, and lives in New York City.

PUBLICATIONS: poems in *Black Dialogue* and *Newark Afro-American Festival Magazine.*

MARGARET WALKER was born in Birmingham, Alabama in 1915. She studied at Northwestern University and received the Master of Arts degree in 1940 from the State University of Iowa. She has taught English at Livingstone College, West Virginia State College, and presently teaches at Jackson State College, Mississippi. Mrs. Alexander in private life, she is the mother of two girls and two boys. She won a Rosenwald Fellowship in 1944.

PUBLICATIONS: her poems have appeared in *Poetry, Opportunity, Creative Writing, American Prefaces;* and in the anthologies *Negro Caravan; Poetry of the Negro; Beyond the Blues; American Negro Poetry.* Her book of poems, *For My People,* was chosen as one of the Yale University Series of

Younger Poets in 1942. Her "Ballad of the Free" was published in the *Broadside Series* in 1966. Her novel of the Civil War and post-Civil War days, *Jubilee,* was a Houghton Mifflin Award novel in 1966.

WORK IN PROGRESS: she is working on her first volume of poems since 1942, tentatively entitled *October Journey.*

SIDELIGHTS: she has recorded some of her poems in *Anthology of Negro Poets* (Folkway Records, FP). Her book *For My People* may be re-issued as a paperback in 1967.

★

REGINALD WILSON was born in Detroit, Michigan, February 24, 1927. He received a B.S. degree from Wayne State University in 1950 and an M.A. in 1959, and is now a doctoral candidate in psychology there. In World War II he served in the Air Force. He is now Federal Project Director at Oakland University in Rochester, Michigan.

PUBLICATIONS: his poems appeared in military service journals at Tuskegee Institute in 1945. He has published several technical papers on psychology in journals such as *Abstracts of the Michigan Academy,* and a sociological study of Negro leadership in the *Negro History Bulletin,* October, 1962.

SIDELIGHTS: "Formerly managing editor of a political journal *(Correspondence)* in which the work of many black Detroit artists and writers appeared. Director of a psychological and educational clinic for the past three years in northwest Detroit. Chairman of the final program of the Grassroots Leadership Conference at King Solomon Baptist Church in Detroit, November, 1963, at which Malcolm X gave his last major speech before leaving the Nation of Islam.

". . . I have tried my hand at attempting to mix images from the deaths of Lincoln and Malcolm, particularly since so much has been made, recently, of the similarity between Lincoln's and Kennedy's death.

"In this freely rendered poem I have adhered strictly to the facts of each assasination [sic]. I have only combined them in such a way as to provide contrast and provoke thought. The title, of course, is taken from the play Lincoln was watching at the time of his death, but its use here is to dedicate the poem to our white fellow Americans."

JOYCE WHITSITT is an English teacher at Northwestern High School in Detroit. She was born August 11, 1938 in Mount Clemens, Michigan, and attended Mount Clemens High School and Wayne University, where she gained a B.S. degree in 1962. The daughter of a Baptist minister, she paid part of her college expenses by singing with dance bands. She was one of the group of Boone House poets associated with Margaret Danner. She is now studying library science at Atlanta University on a fellow-ship.

PUBLICATIONS: poems in *Negro History Bulletin* and *Negro Digest.*

★

JAMES WORLEY was born in 1921 and received an M.A. degree from Columbia University in 1948. During World War II he served in North Africa, Italy, France, and Germany. He is a teacher and lives in Columbia, Indiana.

PUBLICATIONS: poems in *The Reporter, Motive, Prairie Schooner, Christian Century, New Mexico Quarterly, Phylon, Negro Digest, New York Herald Tribune, Quartet, Voices, Western Humanities Review.*

★

JAY WRIGHT was born in Albuquerque, New Mexico, May 25, 1935, and attended the University of California at Berkeley and the graduate school of Rutgers University. He lives in New York City.

PUBLICATIONS: poems in *Freedomways, Negro Digest, Poetry Review, Yale Review, Aphid.*

WORK IN PROGRESS: revision of second play, revision of book of poems.

SIDELIGHTS: "Starting on a second (perhaps the first) book of poems. Book is modelled on Lowell's *Imitations,* using poets of African descent and including source poems from French, Spanish, Portuguese, Arabic and, hopefully, Swahili. Translators are doing literal translations from the last three for me."

Further Reading

BY MALCOLM X

Books

MALCOLM X. *The Autobiography of Malcolm X. With the Assistance of Alex Haley.* New York, Grove Press, 1965.
—*Malcolm X Speaks: Selected Speeches and Statements.* Edited with Prefatory Notes by George Breitman. New York, Merit Publishers, c. 1965.

Pamphlets

MALCOLM X. *Malcolm X Talks to Young People.* New York, The Young Socialist, 1965.
—*Two Speeches by Malcolm X.* New York, Pioneer Publishers 1965.

Periodicals

MALCOLM X. "Angry spokesman Malcolm X Tells Off Whites." *Life* 54:30 May 31, 1963.

—"The Black Struggle in the United States." *Presence Africaine,* English edition, No. 2, 1965.
—"I'm Talking to You, White Man; Excerpt from *Autobiography of Malcolm X,* by Alex Haley and Malcolm X." *Saturday Evening Post* 237:30-2 September 12, 1964.
—"Interview with Malcolm X." A. B. Spellman, *Monthly Review* 16:1 14-24 May, 1964.
—"Interview with Malcolm X." *Young Socialist,* March-April '65.
—"Malcolm X. v. James Farmer: Separation v. Integration. Debate." *Dialogue Magazine,* 1962.
—"Playboy Interview: Malcolm X." Alex Haley. *Playboy* 10:53-4 May, 1963.
—"Racism: The Cancer That Is Destroying America." *Egyptian Gazette,* August 25, 1964.
—"We Are All Blood Brothers." *Liberator,* July, 1964.

Phonograph Records

MALCOLM X. *Message to the Grass Roots from Malcolm X.* Detroit, Afro-American Broadcasting and Recording Company, Suite 503, Tobin Buliding, 1308 Broadway, Detroit, Michigan 48226.
—*Malcolm X Speaks Again.* Twenty Grand Records, (LP-100 vol. 1)

About Malcolm X

Books

BALDWIN, JAMES. *The Fire Next Time.* New York, Dial, 1963.
BENNETT, LERONE, Jr. *Confrontation: Black and White.* Chicago, Johnson Publishing Company, 1965.
BONTEMPS, ARNA and CONROY, JACK. *Anywhere But Here.* New York, Hill and Wang, 1966.
BREITMAN, GEORGE. *The Last Year of Malcolm X: the Evolution of a Revolutionary.* New York, Merit Publishers, 1966.
BRODERICK, FRANCIS L. and MEIER, AUGUST. *Negro Protest Thought in the Twentieth Century.* Indianapolis, Bobbs-Merrill, 1965.
BURNS, W. HAYWOOD. *The Voices of Negro Protest in America.* New York, Oxford University Press, 1963.
CLARK, KENNETH BANCROFT. *The Negro Protest; James Baldwin, Malcolm X, Martin Luther King Talk With Kenneth B. Clark.* Boston, Beacon, 1963.
ESSIEN-UDOM, ESSIEN UDOSEN. *Black Nationalism; a Search for an Identity in America.* Chicago, University of Chicago Press, 1962.
FARMER, JAMES. *Freedom—When?* New York, Random House, 1966.
HERNTON, CALVIN C. *White Papers for White Americans.* New York, Doubleday, 1966.
JONES, LEROI. *Home: Social Essays.* New York, Morrow, 1966.
LINCOLN, CHARLES ERIC. *The Black Muslims in America.* Boston, Beacon Press, 1966.
—*My Face Is Black.* Boston, Beacon Press, 1964.
LOMAX, LOUIS E. *When the Word Is Given; a Report on Elijah Muhammad, Malcolm X, and the Black Muslim world.* Cleveland, World Publishing Company, 1963.
MUHAMMAD, ELIJAH. *Message to the Blackman in America.* Chicago, Muhammad Mosque of Islam No. 2, 1965.
NAGATA, EI. *The Black Revolt: Malcolm X, the Man and His Ideas.* Tokyo, Sanichi Shobo, 1966.
N'DIAYE, JEAN PIERRE. *Les noirs aux Etats-Unis pour les africains,* par J. P. N'Diaye, J. Bassene, B. Poyas. Paris, 1964. (Realites africaines, no. 7).
WARREN, ROBERT PENN. *Who Speaks for the Negro?* New York, Random House, 1965.
WILLIAMS, DANIEL T. and REDDEN, CAROLYN L. *The Black Muslims in the United States: a Selected Bibliography.* Tuskegee, Alabama, Hollis Burke Frissell Library, Tuskegee Institute, 1964.
YEAR. *Year's Pictorial History of the American Negro.* Maplewood, New Jersey, C. S. Hammond, 1965.

Pamphlets

BREITMAN, GEORGE. *Malcolm X, the Man and His Ideas.* New York, Pioneer Publishers, 5 East Third Street, New York, N.Y., March, 1965.

LOUISIANA. LEGISLATURE. JOINT COMMITTEE ON UN-AMERICAN ACTIVITIES. *Activities of "The Nation of Islam" or the Muslim Cult of Islam, in Louisiana.* (Hearing held, November 27, 1962, Baton Rouge, Louisiana) Baton Rouge, 1963.

MITCHELL, SARA. *Brother Malcolm.* New York, Malcolm X Memorial Committee, May, 1965.

VERNON, ROBERT. *The Black Ghetto.* New York, Pioneer Publishers, October, 1964.

WALLACE, MIKE, and LOMAX, LOUIS. "The Hate That Hate Produced." *Newsbeat,* New York: WNTA-TV (July 10, 1958) television program.

Periodicals

ADAMS, ALVIN. "Malcolm X 'Seemed Sincere' About Helping Cause: Mrs. King." *Jet,* March 11, 1965.

ALLEN, ROBERT. "Malcolm X: 2/21/65." *Village Voice,* February 17, 1966.

BALDWIN, JAMES. "Letter from a Region in My Mind." *New Yorker* 88:88, November 17, 1962.

BERGER, MORROE. "Black Muslims." *Horizon 6:48-65* Winter, 1964.

BLACK, PEARL. "Malcolm X Returns." *Liberator,* January '65.

"Black Merchants of Hate." *Saturday Evening Post,* Jan. 26, '63.

BOGGS, JAMES. "Malcolm X Inquiry Stirs Harlem." *Now!* 2:14 January 1966.

BRADLEY, EDWARD. (as told to Louis E. Lomax) "Malcolm X Escaped Killers in Los Angeles by James Bond Ruse." *Paterson Morning Call,* February 25, 1965.

BREITMAN, GEORGE. "The Impact of Malcolm X." *Young Socialist,* March-April, 1966.

—"Going to the UN Can Help, But It's No Cure-All." *The Militant,* March 30, 1964.

—"Malcolm X's Murder and the New York Police," "More Questions on Malcolm X's Murder," and "Why Isn't Daily Press Interested in Who Killed Malcolm X?" *The Militant,* July 12, August 9 and August 23, 1965. (A three-part series raising questions about the assassination.)

—"New Force Can Bring Major Rights Gains" and "His Stand Can Unite and Build Movement." *The Militant,* March 30 and April 6, 1964. (A two-part series appraising the split).

"Brother Malcolm: His Theme Now Is Violence." *U.S. News* 56:19 March 23, 1964.

CAPOUYA, EMIL. "A Brief Return from Mecca." *Saturday Review*, 48:42 November 20, 1965.

CLEAVER, ELDRIDGE. "Letters from Prison." *Ramparts*, August, 1966.

CRAWFORD, MARC. "Ominous Malcolm X Exits from the Muslims." *Life* 56:40—40A March 20, 1964.

"Death and Transfiguration." *Time* 81:23-5, March 8, 1965.

"Death of a Desperado." *Newsweek* 65:24-5 March 8, 1965.

DIAMOND, STANLEY. "The Apostate Muslim." *Dissent*, Spring, 1965.

DOMRESE, ROBERT J. "A Struggle with the Wrong Image." *Harvard Crimson*, May 24, 1966.

DUNAYEVSKAYA, RAYA. "Malcolm X and 'Old Radicals!'" *News and Letters*, April, 1964.

"Enter Muhammed?" *National Review* 14:520, July 2, 1963.

FARMER JAMES. see MALCOLM X. "Malcolm X. v. James Farmer."

GARDNER, JIGS. "The Murder of Malcolm X." *Monthly Review* 16:802-5 April, 1965.

HALL, GORDON D. "Malcolm X: the Man and the Myth." *Boston Sunday Herald*, February 28, 1965.

HAMILTON, BOBB. "El-Hajji Malik Shabazz: Leader, Prophet. Martyr." *Soulbook* 1:81-84. Spring 1965.

HANDLER, M. S. "Malcolm X Splits with Muhammad." *New York Times*, March 9, 1964.

HENRY, LAURENCE. "Malcolm X Lives." *Cavalier*, June, 1966.

HENRY, LAURENCE and RICHARD. "Malcolm X: Behind the Murder Trial." *Now!* 2:7-10 March-April 1966.

HENRY, MILTON R. "New Glory Visits Malcolm X." *Now!* 2:11 March-April 1966.

HENTOFF, NAT. "Elijah in the Wilderness." *Reporter* 23:37-40 August 4, 1960; p. 10, September 29, 1960.

—"Odyssey of a Black Man." *Commonweal*, 183:511-12 January 28, 1966.

HERMAN, DAVID. "Malcolm X Assails U.S. Role in Congo." *The Militant*, December 7, 1964.

HERMAN, DAVID. "Malcolm X Back from Africa — Urges Black United Front." *The Militant*, June 1, 1964.

—"Malcolm X Details Black Nationalist Views." *The Militant*, April 20, 1964.

—"Malcolm X Discusses Bombing of Home." *The Militant*, February 22, 1965.

—"Malcolm X Launches a New Organization." *The Militant*, July 13, 1964.

—"Malcolm X's Last Meeting." *The Militant*, February 22, 1965.

—"3,000 Cheer Malcolm X at Opening Rally in Harlem." *The Militant*, March 30, 1964.

HOLT, LEN. "Malcolm X the Mirror." *Liberator* 6:4-5 Feb. 1966.

HOWE, IRVING. "New Styles in 'Leftism.'" *Dissent*, Summer 1965.

HUNT, FRANK. "Malcolm X Still Lives." *Baltimore Afro-American*, February 19, 1966.

ILLICK, JOSEPH E. "Black Nationalism and the White Press." (A paper delivered to the Association for the Study of Negro Life and History, October 21, 1966, Baltimore.)

ILLO, JOHN. "The Rhetoric of Malcolm X." *The Columbia University Forum* 9:5-12, Spring 1966.

JACKSON, JAMES E. "A Fighting People Forging New Unity." *The Worker,* July 7, 1963. Also appears in *Political Affairs,* August, 1963, under the title, "A Fighting People Forging Unity."

KELLEY, WILLIAM MELVIN. "On Racism, Exploitation and the White Liberal." *Negro Digest,* 22:5-12 January 1967.

JONES, THEODORE. "Malcolm X Knew He Was a 'Marked Man.' " *New York Times,* February 22, 1966.

KEMPTON, MURRAY. "The Fruit of Islam." *New York World-Telegram and Sun,* February 23, 1965.

KIRK, RUSSELL. "Malcolm X's Promise Was Murdered Too." *Detroit Free Press,* March 2, 1965.

KOFSKY, FRANK. "Malcolm X." *Monthly Review,* September, 1966.

KRETZ, T. "Journey Toward Truth." *Christian Century* 82:1513 December 8, 1965.

LARNER, JEREMY. "McComb vs. Harlem." *Dissent,* Spring, 1965.

LEIMAN, MELVIN. "Malcolm X." *Liberation,* April, 1965.

LERNER, MAX. "Malcolm X and "White Devils." *Detroit News,* March 16, 1964.

—"Malcolm's Death." *New York Post,* February 26, 1965.

"Lesson of Malcolm X." *Saturday Evening Post* 237:84 September 12, 1964.

LESTER, JULIUS. "The Angry Children of Malcolm X." *Sing Out!* 16:20-25, October-November 1966.

LIGHTFOOT, CLAUDE. "Negro Nationalism and the Black Muslims." *Political Affairs,* July 1962.

LINCOLN, ERIC C. "Meaning of Malcolm X." *Christian Century* 82:431-3 April 7, 1965.

LOMAX, ALMENA. "Notes on a Nationalist's Death." *The Tribune* (Los Angeles) March 15, 1965.

LUBELL, SAMUEL. "Did Malcolm's Ironic Role Advance Rights?" *Detroit Free Press,* March 1, 1965.

McGILL, RALPH. "Essay on Malcolm X and Black Muslims." *Detroit News,* March 3, 1965.

McMANUS, JANE. "The Outlook of Malcolm X." *National Guardian,* April 18, 1964.

MAJOR, CLARENCE. "Malcolm X the Martyr." 22:37-42, *Negro Digest,* December 1966.

"Malcolm X." *Nation* 200:239 March 8, 1965.

"Malcolm's Brand X." *Newsweek* 63:32 March 23, 1964.

MASSAQUOI, H. J. "Mystery of Malcolm X." *Ebony* 19:38-40 September 1964.

Militant, The (By the Editors). "Murder of Malcolm X Is a Cruel Blow to the Cause of Black Emancipation." March 1, 1965.

MOORE, LOUISE. "When a Black Man Stood Up." *Liberator,* July 1966.

MORRISON, A. "Who Killed Malcolm X?" *Ebony 20:135-6* October 1965.

NADLE, MARLENE. "Malcolm X: The Complexity of a Man in the Jungle." *Village Voice,* February 25, 1965.

NEAL, LAWRENCE P. "Malcolm X and the Conscience of Black America." *Liberator* 6:10-11 February 1966.

—"A Reply to Bayard Rustin — The Internal Revolution." *Liberator,* July 1965.

NELSON, TRUMAN. "Delinquent's Progress." *Nation* 201:336-8 November 8, 1965.

New York Herald Tribune (editorial). "Hate: Full Circle." February 23, 1965.

New York Times (editorial) "Malcolm X." February 22, 1965.

NORDEN, ERIC. "The Murder of Malcolm X." *The Realist,* February, 1967.

"Now It's a Negro Drive for Segregation; Interview." *U.S. News* 56:38-9 March 30, 1964.

"Now It's Negroes vs. Negroes in America's Racial Violence." *U.S. News* 58:6 March 8, 1965.

PARIS, MARTIN. "Negroes Are Willing to Use Terrorism, Says Malcolm X." *Columbia* (University) *Daily Spectator,* February 19, 1965.

PARKS, GORDON. " 'I Was a Zombie Then—Like All Muslims I Was Hypnotized.' " *Life,* March 5, 1965.

"Peking and Malcolm X." *New Republic* 152:8 March 27, 1965; Reply. L. M. Edwards 152:44 April 17, 1965.

PHILLIPS, WALDO B. "Political Implications of Malcolm X's Death." *Los Angeles Herald Dispatch,* March 4, 1965.

"Pied Piper of Harlem." *Christian Century* 81:422 April 1, 1964.

PLIMPTON, G. "Miami Notebook: Cassius Clay and Malcolm X." *Harper's* 228:54-61 June 1964.

PORTER, HERMAN. Nine articles about the Malcolm X murder trial in New York. *The Militant,* January 24, 31; February 7,14, 21, 28; March 7, 14, 21, 1966.

PORTER, RUTH. "Paris Meeting Hears Malcolm X." *The Militant,* December 7, 1964.

PRATTIS, P. L. "Malcolm X Trying to Make Racket Out of Desperation." *Michigan Chronicle,* March 28, 1964.

PROTZ, ROGER. "Millions of Britons See Malcolm X in TV Broadcast of Debate at Oxford." *The Militant,* December 14, 1964.

"Real Reason Why Malcolm X Went to Africa." *Sepia* 13:42-46 October 1964.

REVOLUTIONARY ACTION MOVEMENT (RAM). "Why Malcolm X Died." *Liberator,* April 1965.

FURTHER READING

RING, HARRY. "Radio Interview with Malcolm X." *The Militant* February 8, 1965. (Text of discussion on WBAI-FM, January 28, 1965).

ROBERTSON, BILL. "Elijah Muhammad: America's No. 1 Black Supremacist." *Bronze America* 1:20-25, December 1964.

ROBESON, ESLANDA. "Malcolm X's Funeral, Dignity and Brotherhood." *Baltimore Afro-American,* March 20, 1965.

ROBINSON, JACKIE. "Bullets Silenced a Man of Courage." *Michigan Chronicle,* March 13, 1965.

RUSSELL, CARLOS E. "Exclusive Interview with Brother Malcolm X." *Liberator,* May 1964.

RUSTIN, BAYARD and KAHN, TOM. "The Mark of Oppression." *New America,* March 24, 1965. (Also printed as "The Ambiguous Legacy of Malcolm X," *Dissent* Spring, 1965.)

—"On Malcolm X." *New America,* February 28, 1965.

SAMUELS, GERTRUDE. "Feud Within the Black Muslims." *New York Times Magazine,* p. 17, March 22, 1964

"Satan in the Ghetto." *Newsweek* 66:130 November 15, 1965.

SHABAZZ, JAMES. "Weep for Brother Malcolm, He Is Dead." *The Militant,* March 15, 1965

SHAPIRO, HERBERT. "The Education of Malcolm X." *Jewish Currents* 20:6-11 October 1966.

SOUTHWICK, A. B. "Malcolm X: Charismatic Demagogue; Interview." *Christian Century* 80:740-1 June 5, 1963.

SNELLINGS, ROLLAND. "Malcolm X: As International Statesman." *Liberator* 6:6-9 February 1966.

SPELLMAN, A. B. "Black Nationalism and Radical Unity." *The Second Coming* 1:10-12.

—"The Legacy of Malcolm X." *Liberator* 5:11-13 June 1965.

STRICKLAND, WILLIAM L. "Epitaph for Malcolm X." *Freedom North,* Vol. L, No. 3, 1965.

SYKES, OSSIE. "The Week That Malcolm X Died." *Liberator,* April 1965.

THOMAS, NORMAN. Letter to *Viewpoint* editorial board. *Viewpoint,* June 1965.

"Tragedy of Malcolm X." *America* 112:303 March 6, 1965

"Vendetta by Rivals Feared." *Senior Scholastic* 86:21 March 11, 1965.

VERNON, ROBERT. "Malcolm X, Voice of the Black Ghetto." *International Socialist Review,* Spring 1965.

"Violence versus Non-Violence." *Ebony* 20:168-9 April 1965.

"Violent End of the Man Called Malcolm X; with Report by G. Parks." *Life* 58:26-31 March 5, 1965.

WALKER, WYAT TEE. "Nothing But a Man." *Negro Digest,* August 1965.

WARDE, WILLIAM F. "The Life and Death of Malcolm X." *International Socialist Review* 26:35-7 Spring 1965.

WARREN, ROBERT PENN. "Malcolm X: Mission and Meaning." *Yale Review,* 56:161-171 Winter 1967.

WECHSLER, JAMES A. "About Malcolm X." *New York Post*, February 23, 1965.

—"The Cult of Malcolm X." (Black Nationalist Movement). *Progressive* 28:24-8 June 1964.

—"Malcolm X and the Death of Rev. Klunder." *New York Post*, April 13, 1964.

Weekly People (editorial). "What Killed Malcolm X." March 13, 1965.

"Who Issued the Orders?" *Newsweek* 67:36 March 21, 1966.

"Why Black Muslims Are Focusing on the Nation's Capital Now." *U.S. News* 54:24 May 27, 1963.

"Why Malcolm X Quit the Black Muslims."' *Sepia* 13:58-62 May 1964.

WILEY, C. W. "Who Was Malcolm X?" *National Review* 17:239-40 March 23, 1965.

WILKINS, ROY. "Malcolm X-ism Jars White Complacency." *Detroit News,* January 3, 1965.

—"No Time for Avengers." *New York Amsterdam News.* Mar. 6, 1965.

—"The Repercussions of Malcolm X Death." *Detroit News,* March 7, 1965.

WILLIAMS, ROBERT F. "The Crusader and Mr. Elijah Muhammad." *The Crusader,* May 1963.

—"Malcolm X: Death Without Silence." *The Crusader,* Mar. 1965

WILSON, C. E. "The Quotable Mr. X." *Liberator,* May 1965.

—and SYKES, OSSIE. "Malcolm X: A Tragedy of Leadership." *Liberator,* May 1965.

"Without Malcolm X." *Economist 214:888* February 27, 1965.

WORTHY, WILLIAM. "Malcolm X Says Group Will Stress Politics." *National Guardian,* March 21, 1964.

"X on the Spot." *Newsweek* 62:27 December 16, 1963.

YOUNG, JR., WHITNEY. "Malcolm's Death Solves Nothing." *New York World-Telegram and Sun,* February 25, 1965.

Manuscripts

KELLEY, WILLIAM MELVIN. An unpublished article on the trial of the alleged killers of Malcolm X.

LEAKS, SYLVESTER. A biography of Malcolm X.

APPENDIX

EULOGY OF MALCOLM X
"OUR BLACK MANHOOD . . .
OUR BLACK SHINING PRINCE! . . ."

Here — at this final hour, in this quiet place, Harlem has come to bid farewell to one of its brightest hopes — extinguished now, and gone from us forever.

For Harlem is where he worked and where he struggled and fought — his home of homes, where his heart was, and where his people are — and it is, therefore, most fitting that we meet once again — in Harlem — to share these last moments with him.

For Harlem has been ever gracious to those who have loved her, have fought for her and have defended her honor even to the death. It is not in the memory of man that this beleaguered, unfortunate but nonetheless proud community has found a braver, more gallant young champion than this Afro-American who lies before us — unconquered still.

I say the word again, as he would want me to: Afro-American — Afro-American Malcolm, who was a master, was most meticulous in his use of words. Nobody knew better than he the power words have over the minds of men. Malcolm had stopped being "Negro" years ago.

It had become too small, too puny, too weak a word for him, Malcolm was bigger than that. Malcolm had become an Afro-American and he had wanted — so desperately — that we, that all his people would become Afro-Americans too.

There are those who will consider it their duty, as friends of the Negro people, to tell us to revile him, to flee even from the presence of his memory, to save ourselves by writing him out of the history of our turbulent times.

Many will ask what Harlem finds to honor in this stormy, controversial and bold young captain — and we will smile.

Many will say turn away — away from this man, for he is not a man but a demon, a monster, a subverter and an enemy of the black man — and we will smile.

They will say that he is of hate — a fanatic, a racist — who can only bring evil to the cause for which you struggle!

And we will answer and say unto them: Did you ever talk to Brother Malcolm? Did you ever touch him, or have him smile at you? Did you ever really listen to him? Did he ever do a mean thing? Was he ever himself associated with violence or any public disturbance? For if you did you would know him. And if you knew him you would know why we must honor him: Malcolm was our manhood, our living black manhood! This was his meaning to his people. And, in honoring him, we honor the best in ourselves.

Last year, from Africa, he wrote these words to a friend: "My Journey," he says, "is almost ended, and I have a much

broader scope than when I started out, which I believe will add
new life and dimension to our struggle for freedom and honor,
and dignity in the States. I'm writing these things so that you
will know for a fact the tremendous sympathy and support we
have among the African States for our Human Rights Struggle.
The main thing is that we keep a United Front wherein our most
valuable time and energy will not be wasted fighting each other."

However much we differed with him — or with each other
about him and his value as a man, let his going from us serve
only to bring us together, now. Consigning these mortal remains
to earth, the common mother of all, secure in the knowledge
that what we place in the ground is no more now a man — but
a seed — which, after the winter of discontent — will come forth
again to meet us. And we shall know him then for what he was
and is — a Prince — our own black shining Prince! — who didn't
hesitate to die, because he loved us so.

OSSIE DAVIS

INDEX OF AUTHORS

(Boldface type indicates by, lightface indicates about)

INDEX OF POEMS

BROADSIDE SERIES—SINGLE POEMS

50c Each ($6.00 a year)

Portfolio for Broadsides
1. Ballad of Birmingham, Dudley Randall
2. Dressed All in Pink, Dudley Randall
3. Gabriel, Robert Hayden
4. Ballad of the Free, Margaret Walker
5. The Sea Turtle and The Shark, M. B. Tolson
7. A Poem for Black Hearts, LeRoi Jones
8. Booker T. and W. E. B., Dudley Randall
9. A Child's Nightmare, Bobb Hamilton
11. Sunny, Naomi Long Madgett
12. Letter from a Wife, Carolyn Reese
14. Race Results, U.S.A., 1966, Sarah W. Fabio
15. Song of The Son, Jean Toomer
16. Back Again, Don L. Lee
17. The Black Narrator, Le Graham
18. Black Madonna, Harold Lawrence
19. The Wall, Gwendolyn Brooks
20. At That Moment, Raymond Patterson
21. 2 Poems for Black Relocation Centers, Knight
22. Not Light, Nor Bright, Nor Feathery, Danner
23. At Bay, James A. Emanuel
24. Earth, Askia Muhammad Toure'
28. Black and White, Tony Rutherford
31. T.C. (Terry Callier, True Christian), Bradford
32. Ginger Bread Mama, Doughtry Long
33. One Sided Shout-Out, Don L. Lee
35. Granny Blak Poet, Arthur Pfister
36. For Black Poets Who Think of Suicide, Knight
37. Now Ain't That Love?, Carolyn Rodgers

38. Slaughterhouse, Helen Pulliam
39. County Jail, Jill Witherspoon
40. Rip-Off, Ronda Davis
41. All I Gotta Do, Nikki Giovanni
42. Goodnight, Paula Alexander
43. Muslim Men, Sterling Plumpp
44. Long Rap, Carolyn Rodgers
45. The Nigger Cycle, K. A. Mwandishe
46. A Simple Poem To Mae, O. K .Tarajia
47. Black Henry, Rockie Taylor
48. Two Poems, Robert Keeby & Stephany
49. Tears and Kisses, J. Amaker, G. Gracia, P. Kirk-
   wood, L. Lunford, & W. Rutledge, Jr.
50. For H. W. Fuller, Carolyn Rodgers
51. Poems, Bobb Hamilton, George Buggs
52. Poems, Yusuf, J. Smith, R. Bowen, C. Clemmons
53. Poems, H. Kinamo, L. Tolbert, B. Rogers,
   A. Kingcade
54. Poems, L. Riley, T. Washington, Jr., Robert. L.,
   M. Khalilmalik
55. Black Song, J. D. Perry
56. Black Gifts for a Black Child, Shango
57. Gonna Free Him, Evelyn Clarke
58. Three Poems, Carl Carter
59. A Hip Tale in the Death Style, J. Amini
60. Five Poems, Alice Walker
61. Four Poems, J. P. Randall, R. Oxford, J. Forsh
62. Green Apples, Dudley Randall

BROADSIDE VOICES

Broadside Album: Rappin' and Readin', by Don L. Lee $5.00
Broadside on Broadway: Seven Poets Read (cassette) 5.00
Tapes of poets reading their own books (reels and cassettes) 5.00

Tapes by Emanuel, Giovanni, Jeffers, Hodges, Knight, Randall, Arnez & Murphy, Sanchez, Eckels, Marvin X, Stephany, Lee, Kgositsile, Walker, Danner, Brooks, Major

---

BROADSIDE POSTERS

1. For Black Poets Who Think of Suicide, by Etheridge Knight; illus. by Talita Long $1.00
2. On Getting a Natural, by Dudley Randall; illus. by Leonard Baskin 1.00
   (50 signed by poet and artist) each 10.00
3. Black Silhouette, by Pat Whitsitt 1.00
4. Angela, by Talita Long 1.00
5. Protect the Sister, by Reginald Payne & Pearl Eckles 2.00

THE BLACK POSITION—A PERIODICAL (Annual) $1.00

BROADSIDE POETS

Against the Blues, by Alvin Aubert. 0-910296-73-1 .... paper $1.50
Aloneness (children's), by Gwendolyn Brooks. .... Cloth 0-910296-75-8 $3.00 paper 0-910296-55-3 1.00
Beer Cans, Bullets, Things & Pieces, by Arthur Pfister. 0-910296--29-4 .... 1.25
Black Arts: An Anthology of Black Creations, Edited by Ahmed Alhamisi and Harun Kofi Wangara.
  (Black Arts Publications) 910296-06-5 .... 3.50
Black Feeling, Black Talk, by Nikki Giovanni. 910296-31-6 .... 1.00
Black Judgement, by Nikki Giovanni. 910296-07-3 .... 1.50
Black Love Black Hope, by Doughtry Long. 0-910296-20-0 .... 1.00
Black Man Listen, by Marvin X. 910296-08-1 .... tape $5.00, book 1.00
  Poems and Proverbs voice the philosophy of the Nation of Islam.
Black Poetry: A Supplement to Anthologies Which Exclude Black Poets,
  Edited by Dudley Randall. 910296-09-X .... cloth $4.00, paper   .95
Black Pride, by Don L. Lee. 910296-04-9 .... 1.00
  The second book by the impressive young Chicago poet.
Black Velvet, by Everett Hoagland. 910296-34-0 .... 1.00
Black Wisdom, by Frenchy Jolene Hodges. 0-910296-40-5 .... tape $5.00, paper 1.00
Black Words, by Arthur Boze. 0-910296-39-1 .... paper 1.00
Blues For Mama, by John Raven. 0-910296-54-5 50
The Broadside Annual, 1972, ed. Jill Witherspoon. 0-910296-77-4 .... Paper 1.00
A Broadside Treasury, 1965-1970, Edited by Gwendolyn Brooks.
                              cloth 0-910296-53-7 $6.00, paper 0-910296-51-0 4.00
Cities Burning, by Dudley Randall. 910296-10-3 .... tape $5.00, book 1.00
  Reflects the troubled emotions and tragic events of our time.
The Cotton Club, by Clarence Major. 0-910296-62-6 .... tape $5.00, paper 1.50
Directionscore: Selected and New Poems, by Don L. Lee.
         paper ISBN 0-910296-48-8 $3.75, cloth 0-910296-49-0 $6.00 Special Edition 0-910296-50-2 15.00
Don't Ask Me Who I Am, by James Randall, Jr. 910296-46-4 .... 1.00
Don't Cry, Scream, by Don L. Lee. 910296-11-1 .... tape $5.00, cloth $4.50, paper 1.50
  A brilliant, devastating book by a leading young poet.
Down Nigger Paved Streets, by William A. Thigpen, Jr. 0-910296-74-X .... paper 1.00
Dynamite Voices: Black Poets of the 1960's, by Don L. Lee. ISBN 0-910296-33-2 .... 2.75
East 110th Street, by Jose-Angel Figeroa, 0-910296-53-3 .... 1.50
Family Pictures, by Gwendolyn Brooks. 910296-43-X .... tape $5.00, cloth $5.00, paper 1.00
For Malcolm: Poems on the Life and the Death of Malcolm X, Edited by Dudley Randall and
  Margaret Burroughs. 910296-12-X .... cloth $4.95, paper 2.95
Frank, by Carolyn Thompson (a children's book). 910296-41-3 .... 1.00
Guerilla Warfare, by Ahmed Alhamisi. (Black Arts Publications) 1.00
Holy Ghosts, by Ahmed Akinwole Alhamisi. ...... cloth 0-910296-70-7, $4.50, paper 0-910296-38-3 1.95
Home Is Where the Soul Is, by Jon Eckels. 910296-00-6 .... tape $5.00, book 1.00
  A young California poet who is together and relevant.
Homecoming, by Sonia Sanchez. 910296-05-7 .... tape $5.00, book 1.00
  A passionate, earthy first book by a gifted poet.
Impressions of African Art, by Margaret Danner. 910296-13-8 .... 1.00
It's A New Day (a children's book), by Sonia Sanchez. 0-910296-60-X ...... Cloth $4.00, paperback 1.25
Jump Bad: a New Chicago Anthology, Edited by Gwendolyn Brooks. 0-910296-32-2 .... paper 4.00
Life Styles, by Marion Alexander Nicholes. ISBN 0-910296-36-7 .... 1.00
More to Remember: Poems of Four Decades, by Dudley Randall. (Third World Press)
                              cloth 0-910296-59-6 $5.00, paper 0-910296-58-8 1.95
Moving Deep, by Stephany. 910296-18-9 .... tape $5.00, book 1.00
  Love poems by a young new poet and artist.
My Blackness Is the Beauty of This Land, by Lance Jeffers. 910296-28-6 .... tape $5.00, paper 1.00
Our Business in the Streets, by Jon Eckels. ISBN 0-910296-31-6 .... paper 1.00
Panther Man, by James A. Emanuel. 910296-35-9 .... tape $5.00, paper 1.00
Poem Counterpoem, by Margaret Danner and Dudley Randall. 910296-14-6 ...... tape $5.00, book 1.00
  A unique arrangement of paired poems by two poets of longstanding distinction.
Poems From Prison, by Etheridge Knight. 910296-15-4 .... tape $5.00, paper 1.00
Prophets for a New Day, by Margaret Walker. 910296-21-9 .... tape $5.00, paper 1.00
Re:Creation, by Nikki Giovanni. 910296-47-2 .... tape $5.00, cloth $4.50, paper 1.50
Riot, by Gwendolyn Brooks. 910296-19-7 .... cloth $5.00, paper 1.00
A Safari of African Cooking, by Bill Odarty. ..... cloth 0-910296-72-3 $5.95, paper 0-910296-63-4 3.95
Saint Nigger, by C. E. Cannon. 910296-45-6 .... paper 1.00
Singing Sadness Happy, by Lyn. 0-910296-71-5 .... 1.50
Song for Nia, by Doughtry Long. 0-910296-64-2 .... paper 1.50
Spirits Unchained, by Keorapetse Kgositsile. 910296-01-4 .... tape $5.00, book 1.00
Sugarfields, by Barbara Mahone. (Distributed by Broadside Press) 1.25
The Rocks Cry Out, by Beatrice M. Murphy and Nancy L. Arnez. 910296-16-2 ... tape $5.00, book 1.00
The Treehouse and Other Poems, by James A. Emanuel. 910296-17-0 .... tape $5.00, book 1.00
  Terse lyrics by widely published young poet.
Think Black, by Don L. Lee. 910296-03-0 .... 1.00
We a BaddDDD People, by Sonia Sanchez. 910296-27-8 .... tape $5.00, paper 1.50
We Don't Need No Music, by Pearl Cleage Lomax. ISBN: 0-910296-61-8; LCN: 70-156400 .... 1.00
We the Black Woman, by Femi Funmi Ifetayo. (Black Arts Publications) 1.00
We Walk the Way of the New World, by Don L. Lee. 910296-26-X .. tape $5.00, cloth $4.50, paper 1.50
  Don Lee's fourth book is "softer, but louder."
The Youth Makes the Revolution, by Sonebeyatta Amungo (Black Arts Publications) 1.00